Master the
Mystery of
Human Nature

Master the Mystery of Mystery of Human Nature

Resolving the Conflict of Opposing Values

D. Scott Frettenero

TRUE DIRECTIONS
AN AFFILIATE OF TARCHER BOOKS

iUniverse®

MASTER THE MYSTERY OF HUMAN NATURE
RESOLVING THE CONFLICT OF OPPOSING VALUES

iUniverse books may be ordered through booksellers or by contacting:

iUniverse
1663 Liberty Drive
Bloomington, IN 47403
www.iuniverse.com
1-800-Authors (1-800-288-4677)

Because of the dynamic nature of the Internet, any web addresses or links contained in this book may have changed since publication and may no longer be valid. The views expressed in this work are solely those of the author and do not necessarily reflect the views of the publisher, and the publisher hereby disclaims any responsibility for them.

Any people depicted in stock imagery provided by Thinkstock are models, and such images are being used for illustrative purposes only. Certain stock imagery © Thinkstock.

This book contains copyrighted materials of Wilson Learning Worldwide, Inc. © Wilson Learning Worldwide, Inc.

Myers-Briggs® and Myers-Briggs Type Indicator® are registered trademarks of the Myers-Briggs Indicator Trust in the United States and other countries.

ISBN: 978-1-4917-6623-1 (sc)
ISBN: 978-1-4917-6622-4 (e)

Library of Congress Control Number: 2015906122

Print information available on the last page.

iUniverse rev. date: 9/16/2015

Contents

Part 1
Understanding Humanity

Part 2
A Path toward Mastery

Preface

The science of the mind can only have for its proper goal the understanding of human nature by every human being, and through its use, brings peace to every human soul.
—Alfred Adler, *Understanding Human Nature*

This is a book about understanding human nature. I have to believe that human nature is one of the biggest unsolved mysteries of our existence. It is a topic that is as vast as it is unknown to the majority of us.

If you ask anyone to try to explain what he or she knows about human nature, be prepared to receive a blank stare and possibly some incoherent babble. It is such an enormous and mysterious subject that virtually no one will know where to begin. The *Merriam-Webster* dictionary defines human nature as "the ways of thinking, feeling, and acting that are common to most people." But what do any of us really and truly know about it?

It isn't taught in school. There aren't many popular books about human nature to read and learn from. It isn't discussed on TV or radio talk shows. I'll bet most people can't remember ever talking about it. But for cripes' sake, isn't it the most fundamental aspect of our lives? Most of us can't really and truly understand ourselves. And we don't have a clue why others do what they do.

I think that most of us can agree that life is a mystery here on planet Earth, where the billions of people live their lives day to day, most not knowing what their purpose is. We can't figure out life's answers because some of us don't even know the questions to ask. It can be so confusing—sometimes even a bit maddening.

In our present-day world, human interaction on all levels is something that we can clearly acknowledge could be improved. Just read the papers or watch the news. There is so much chaos, turmoil, and confusion in the world today. It is easy to see that there is a great deal of frustration and exasperation with our inabilities to work through it all.

Somehow I get a sense that the world is ready and ripe for new solutions to overcome the problems that are facing us as individuals, as families, as communities, and as nations. Maybe now is the time for some of us to discover an improved way of thinking and feeling about ourselves and our interactions with others. (As the dictionary tells us, this is the definition of human nature.) This book was written for that very purpose.

The development of this book had its origin when I began my attempts to overcome my inabilities to understand myself and those around me. Some of my conclusions and philosophies about people and the world in general weren't working too well. The results I was getting were not what I was wanting. I needed to make some changes.

Then, when I finally married, it became perfectly clear that I also didn't have the foggiest notion about members of the opposite sex. This was a real problem. I had to become a serious student of this human nature subject because my particular partner of the opposite sex was totally opposite of me in every way imaginable.

I had ventured into waters that seemed uncharted, and I became engrossed in trying to figure out how to have a great relationship despite the fact that my bride and I were so very different in our wants and ways. It was a real challenge, but down deep, I felt there was a pot of gold at the end of that rainbow.

In the midst of working through the problems of a new marriage, I had to become very adept in the art of soul-searching, philosophizing, and ultimately conflict resolution. My relationship became a means for personal growth, and it helped elevate my awareness of certain aspects of life that I previously didn't have a clue existed. I began to learn that what I didn't know far outweighed what I thought I knew.

As time went on, the experiences I had in life took me in some very weird and wonderful directions that ultimately led me to want to write it down in a book. It seemed to me that what I was learning was too good not to share with others. So share I shall!

I don't claim authorship to most of the principles that will be presented here. I am just organizing them in such a way that I hope will make as much sense to you as it did to me. I promise you that the material will be nonjudgmental. There will be no preaching or telling you how to live your life, just some solid information that might enhance it.

As you read on, you will note that each chapter of this book is called a lesson. I have to believe that learning life's lessons is mandatory for its mastery. There will be no homework or formal tests given, as life already does that perfectly for us. Life is our classroom with never-ending problems given to us as our assignments. We can stubbornly refuse to do our work, but a flunking grade seems to always mean we have to repeat our lessons. Learning about human nature will hopefully help move you to the front of the class.

At the end of each lesson, I have attempted to summarize its messages with a poem. Never having written poetry before, my intention is that you will be able to grasp the subject matter in a more subjective way. It was done to create a feeling for what is written in each lesson.

I hope this book helps you in whatever way is right for you. There is so much to cover. Let's begin.

Acknowledgments

Most of all, I wish to give credit where it is certainly due for the wonderful work and research done on temperament types by Isabel Myers, Katharine Briggs, David Keirsey, Marilyn Bates, and many others who have contributed so much to the understanding of this vital subject. In truth, these people literally changed my life by reshaping how I looked at people. I cannot over-emphasize the importance of this in helping me create this book.

Next, I want to thank Dr. Robert Quinn, developer of the Competing Values Model, the model that put everything into perspective for me and was the spark that started this monumental project.

I also wish to thank those who enlightened me and helped me grow in so many ways, including Dr. William Glasser, a world-renowned psychiatrist; Napoleon Hill, for his ever-relevant and groundbreaking works; and Helen Schucman, for *A Course in Miracles*, which explains how the ego works, the true meaning of forgiveness, and so much more. Thank you all!

In memory, I also acknowledge the creativity, expertise, and assistance of my dear friend George A. Scott. He was my mentor, teacher, and confidant. We spent many hours brainstorming and collaborating on our projects. I really miss him, his vast experience, and our friendship.

Lastly, I thank my wonderful and beautiful wife, who by her nature, taught me how to live, learn, and love. Without her, this book and my life would be empty and meaningless.

—D. Scott Trettenero

Introduction

We have pretty well finished the geographic exploration of the earth; we have pushed the scientific exploration of nature, both lifeless and living, to a point at which its main outlines have become clear; but the exploration of human nature and its possibilities has scarcely begun. A vast New World and its possibilities awaits its Columbus.
—Julian Huxley, *Transhumanism*

You are about to enter a sphere of knowledge that has up until now been largely foreign to anyone outside scientific and academic circles. This is unfortunate because once you understand some basics of human nature, you will understand yourself, others, and life as never before. Further, if it were to become common knowledge (and that is the aim of this book), we would all benefit in ways too far reaching to even contemplate.

Yet it is easy to predict what it can do for your world. And as just stated, if you read what you see on the pages that follow, you will indeed gain a new appreciation of human nature and why you and I do what we do. And some critically important pathways will be discussed that can lead to an enhanced and happier way of being.

If you decide to act upon the knowledge in this book, I can flat-out guarantee that you will be much better for it. Doing that, your benefits can include

- understanding the roots of human conflicts that plague us all;
- learning where you and others fit in this world;
- discovering secrets of successful relationships;
- recognizing the paradox of life that has entrapped humanity for eons; and
- rising above it all to enjoy a happier, more-productive life.

With the proven information presented in this book, things that used to be a mystery to you will suddenly make sense. You'll discover that there is an order to human nature. The mystical will become practical. The nonsensical will become clear.

Very likely, you will experience a sense of calm and freedom in recognizing the beauty and wonder of how human nature reflects the balance of powers in our world.

If all this sounds like too much to swallow, please hold judgment at this time. I ask that you open your mind and set aside your cynicism for now. As you will soon see, applying the basic principles set forth in this book can be a huge blessing for you and those around you.

A word of warning: some of what will be covered might seem at first glance to be oversimplification or totally obvious. I ask that you bear with me in these cases because I have found some of these things that appear that way are more profound than you might think.

This book is going to help you rediscover some of the wisdom of the ages, which will be presented in a new way. There is a lot of information to process that will go against some of our present-day conventional thinking. Some of it may even be unsettling to ponder.

Please consider what Albert Einstein, a rather bright individual, had to say about the present state of our human experience and the direction we need to go to overcome it. I believe that in just a few sentences he has encapsulated everything that will be covered in this book.

> A human being is part of a whole, called by us the Universe, a part limited in time and space. He experiences himself, his thoughts and feelings, as something separated from the rest—a kind of optical delusion of the consciousness. This delusion is a kind of prison for us, restricting us to our personal desires and to affection for a few people nearest us. Our task must be to free ourselves from this prison by widening our circles of compassion to embrace all living creatures and the whole of nature in its beauty.
>
> Letter of 1950 quoted in *New York Times* (29 March 1972)

If you read this quote very carefully, you may understand the genius in his message, and very likely, you will nod in agreement. But the problem with Einstein's observation is that he tells us what we need to do, but he doesn't offer any suggestions for how to go about doing it. It is all theoretical with no practical applications. We need some real help here, Mr. Einstein, right now!

There are a number of great teachings from the past that are here to help us. But most are not that easy to fully understand and are open to many different interpretations. This creates a lot of confusion about the meaning of life and how we should live it.

There is so much conflict in the world as confused people fight each other over who is right about their different misinterpretations. It is obvious that our inability to get along with each other extracts a huge toll on society, which is evidenced by our ridiculously high divorce rate, wars and threats of wars, unhappy kids and frustrated parents, widespread intolerance of another point of view in politics and elsewhere, road rage, school shootings, and domestic violence.

So What Is This All About?

Master the Mystery of Human Nature is about simplifying the complex nature of this subject in order to understand how and why people do what they do. Understanding ourselves is the first step in this process. Understanding others is next.

Then, learning about the inherent conflicts of our temperaments is critically imperative. Recognizing why there is so much conflict and how it's built in to our system is enlightening beyond imagination.

How to rise above it all in order to regain a little sanity, which we all need in today's crazy world, will be discussed in full detail so this mystery will not be so mysterious.

One of the reasons for writing this book was to begin the process of deciphering this vital subject so we can rise beyond our present-day incomprehension and break free from these shackles of unawareness. Solving a problem like human nature has been beyond the reach of most of us because it is so mysterious. A problem this enormous requires a new perspective on life.

A problem, any problem, cannot be solved or reduced until its cause is understood. Most of us really don't have a clue about our own basic human nature, so how can we possibly solve any problems related to it?

M. Scott Peck, author of *The Road Less Traveled,* helps us look at problems in a new way. In his book, he says, "It is only because of problems that we grow mentally and spiritually." I will personally guarantee that if you can intellectually and emotionally grasp the information this book has to offer, you will grow mentally and spiritually.

It follows that the only way to make any significant reduction of our all-too-common human tragedies on a personal, community, and national level is to help as many people as possible understand some basic knowledge about human nature and the problems associated with being human.

I believe this easy-to-understand book will be a giant step in that direction.

What It Can Do for You Personally

Learning some of human nature's secrets can bring huge benefits to your personal, professional, and family life. You will be able to uncover the real you in terms of your predetermined temperament, which helps explain how you view and experience life—your built-in biases, values, strengths, and limitations. You will be able to finally understand and appreciate people who are different from you.

Most importantly, you will develop an awareness of yourself and understand why and how you do what you do. Becoming objectively aware of the self can unleash enormous possibilities in our lives. Awareness of self can actually change our perceptions of how we see our selves and our relationships with others. We can gain control over our feelings and not be so reactive and impulsive when the world doesn't go the way we would like.

An unawareness of how our selves operate translates into being unconscious in many of our actions and behaviors. Self-awareness becomes a means to gain a clear perspective of your personality, including your strengths and weaknesses. It also helps you understand others and how they react to you because of how you are.

This book will help you deal with the conflicts we all face as humans. Conflicts that have haunted you for years might be resolved, and new conflicts may be prevented.

Your career can be enhanced when you are given the tools to deal with people more effectively. Marriage can take on a whole new meaning and become far happier. Your children will definitely benefit from your new and improved perspective of parenting. It might keep you from ruining their lives and keep them from ruining yours … and much, much more. That's a lot to promise, but read on to find out for yourself.

Why This Book Is Special

It is no secret that self-help books are numerous and easy to find on the shelves of bookstores and online retailers. Most of them are wonderful in their own ways and can have great value. But books that specifically address human nature and describe it in easy-to-understand terminology are few and far between. Most of the literature is written in philosophical and intellectual jargon that is difficult to read and comprehend.

At this point, you might be asking yourself some of these questions:

- If this is such an important subject and so essential to every person on this planet, why have so few people taken the time and energy to write about it and discuss it?
- If knowing and understanding this subject is so vital to solving problems that plague each and every one of us (and it is), why isn't it common knowledge?
- If it's as critical to understanding and getting along with others as said, why hasn't somebody made it easy to understand and apply to your life?

Well, finally, somebody has. This book translates the tremendously important, yet complex work of philosophers, psychologists, scientists, and other pioneers in this field into something that is easy to immediately apply to our lives. Also, it does it without diluting the essential and proven truth of the material.

Yet, it does much more than that. This book takes the work of others and combines the information to create a new matrix that better explains how and why people are different and how the world really works because of our differences. You will learn how the conflicting values and dualities of the physical world are mirrored by human nature. As you will see, there is an order and method to all the madness we experience.

This book can prove to be invaluable to anyone and everyone who has ever wondered about the mysteries of being human and the lives we experience.

Isn't it a shame?
The answers we can't find,
Regarding human nature.
The blind still lead the blind.

Without a map or guide.
Which path should we choose?
Stumbling through the maze,
Its purpose to confuse.

This labyrinth obscures our vision,
Our reflection is all we glimpse.
If we could rise above it,
It would all make perfect sense

Part 1

Understanding Humanity

Lesson 1

A World of Conflict

If we can stay with the tension of opposites long enough—sustain it, be true to it—we can sometimes become vessels within which the divine opposites come together and give birth to a new reality.
—Marie-Louise von Franz, *The Art of Original Thinking*

We are going to begin our exploration of the mysteries of human nature with a concept that is so profound and pervasive in our lives that it permeates everything we think, feel, and do. In order to illustrate this important concept, we will start by contrasting a few common sayings that have been handed down for generations. Even though these groups of sayings are opposing and conflicting in nature, each portrays a snippet of life that we have all experienced to be true in certain situations.

BIRDS OF A FEATHER FLOCK TOGETHER **OPPOSITES ATTRACT**	**THE MORE THE MERRIER** **TWO'S COMPANY, THREE'S A CROWD**
NOTHING VENTURED, NOTHING GAINED **BETTER SAFE THAN SORRY**	**WITH AGE COMES WISDOM** **OUT OF THE MOUTH OF BABES...**

1

How can each of these groups of opposite statements be true when they represent opposing views? The fact of the matter is they are. You might ask yourself, "So what?" Well, to begin with, much of our misunderstandings and conflict in the world stem from our lack of knowledge illustrated by these four simple, conflicting groups of sayings.

When you look at the sets of opposing sayings, you can see that they are completely invalidating of each other. But I am sure you will agree that each of these statements is true in certain situations. So both are true, yet they are opposing in nature. Can you see that there is some potential for conflict here?

A common human problem we face is that conflict can easily and readily appear when someone's beliefs are the exact opposite of someone else's, especially when the beliefs have an emotional attachment. There is conflict everywhere you turn: conflict between nations, factions within nations, spouses, family members, employees and employers, and just everyday people in general. It is no stretch to say that the results can be catastrophic—in wars, riots, suicides, divorce, and untold heartache.

So what is the solution to our universal problem of conflict and turmoil? I believe that it begins with the knowledge and understanding of the concept that basic human nature is built on opposing and competing differences within each and every one of us. This is the source of most of the trouble in this world.

Can it be that basic—and that serious? There is absolutely no question that it is. This book will help show you that instead of all this confusion, we can ultimately find glory in our differences. Our conflicts play an integral part in reaching our lofty goals. We will be exploring this in detail.

It would appear that our present-day solution to disagreements based upon conflicting beliefs is to stand up and fight for our sides. Sometimes even to the death. Is there a better way? Of course there is! Read on to find out just how to do it.

Many books have already been written on pieces and parts of this subject, but this critically important information has not become a component of common culture. Maybe it is because these books have been written by scientists or intellectuals in such a manner that only other scientists or intellectuals can fully appreciate them.

How sad and unfortunate for us all.

Humankind has achieved so much in so many areas of life that it's unnecessary to even mention the high points. Yet for all our spectacular accomplishments, basic human nature, which is at the core of our existence and the source of our experiences in this world, seems to remain a mystery for most of us.

What is going on here? How can this be? It seems that all we really know about human nature is that we are all very different for some strange unknown reason. If we are all human beings who share a common nature, why are we so dissimilar in so many ways? How is it that some people feel, think, and act so completely opposite from the way you do? That is exactly what we are about to explore.

I Didn't Have a Clue.

I used to be unable to understand or relate to most people. (This is the main reason why I became interested in this subject.) I just couldn't figure them out, and at that point in time I really didn't want to. I came to the only conclusion that made sense to me. I truly believed that most people in the world were weird, crazy, or stupid. From my way of thinking, it was the only rational decision to come to.

Only a small circle of friends, family members, and other people who thought like I did accounted for what I considered to be somewhat normal, functioning human beings. And these were the people I felt comfortable being with. As for the others, my dealings with them usually ended up with poor results because I just couldn't see things their way—and they definitely couldn't see things my way. Do you feel—or have you ever felt—like this?

As I grew older and somewhat more experienced associating with people, I began observing them and myself more closely. Being in the business world, I had to deal with all kinds of people in a variety of ways. Because of my inabilities to be effective with people in my personal life, I found that I was also ineffective in my business life.

When you own your own business, you learn that you are responsible for the business's results. And I wasn't too happy with the results I was getting. I decided to try to modify some of my behaviors as I finally understood that most of my business problems were *me*. I began to investigate areas that led me to some revelations and transformations. Before that, I didn't have a clue what a screw-up I was when it came to my understanding of self and my relationship to others. I was just doing what felt right to me.

Life is so full of turmoil and heartache because we don't understand each other. And we can usually find it close to home. What about your own family? Do sparks fly when some of your in-laws get together? Do you have family members who haven't talked to each other in years? Or is there at least one black sheep in the family who no one can figure out or help? Could much of our confusion, pain, and resulting turmoil be avoided with some basic knowledge of human nature? Yes! But it seems that this kind of knowledge isn't available to most of us.

How about one of the biggest travesties in our culture: divorce? Every family seems to have been affected by this one. What is going on here? What are we doing about it? Men and women are obviously different from each other in the way they think, feel, and act. But does that mean there is no way to solve this problem when more than 50 percent of marriages end badly? I am certain there is a way. Again, it begins with knowledge about human nature that presently isn't made known to the general public.

These are just a few examples of the seemingly endless array of situations we experience as human beings because we don't understand each other. We all have our own stories to tell of our inability to get along with another. And we are all victims of indiscretions on a fairly regular basis. None of us are immune. You would think that the universal nature of human conflict would warrant some attention. For some strange reason, this hasn't happened.

Our inability to understand and appreciate the differences between us can lead to problems, which affect us deeply in many ways. A lack of knowledge about human nature influences self-esteem, self-confidence, direction, and finding a purpose in life.

What's Wrong With Men? What's Wrong With Women?

One of the most common problems we face is the inability to understand our counterparts of the opposite sex. So much of human conflict is based upon our mutual lack of understanding of each other. Why does it have to be that way? Why are we so inherently different?

Many a TV sitcom has its storyline based on this kind of conflict. You've laughed at those funny observations of this never-ending comedy/tragedy, but it is not so funny when you are in a heated argument with your significant other.

There was a time in my life when my inability to relate to women caused me much tribulation. I didn't have the slightest inkling how or why they were like they were. And I had absolutely no skills in dealing with them. Needless to say, I didn't have much success in this department. I considered them very complicated and frustrating. My relationships were at best superficial and at worst a disaster. I ended up being single much longer than was acceptable to most mothers, including my own.

Then I met a beautiful and intoxicating woman who totally knocked me off my feet! I believe Thumper in the *Bambi* movie called it "twitterpated." I didn't know what had hit me, and I sure wasn't prepared for what was in store for me.

When I came out from under the ether, my life was completely turned upside down. I had to deal with an incredibly headstrong woman who had a completely different viewpoint on life, and she was very comfortable telling me how she saw it. Man, was I in for it!

She turned out to be the opposite of me in every way imaginable. It was amazing how opposite two people could be. I was in the boot camp of conflict-resolution training without a manual. It was anything but easy for me to deal with this woman, mainly because of my inabilities. I learned in the hardest ways possible. But I did eventually learn—and I am still learning.

In reality, conflict is built into every aspect of this world—not just with people. Think about it. There are opposing forces working at all times in our external physical environments.

Which Is Best—Day or Night?

Aren't day and night opposites and conflicting in nature? How about wet and dry or hot and cold? They aren't just opposites and conflicting; they are complementary in their ways. Which one is more important: day or night? Neither is, of course.

If it were daylight all the time, the earth would become a baked, barren, parched desert. There would be no water for lakes, streams, or oceans. With constant night and no sunlight, the Earth would become a frozen wasteland with no plants, flowers, or trees. With only constant day or night, the planet would not support life. Put the two in balance—and look at the results. It is the same with other opposing forces.

Take the seasons, for example. Which is the best one: spring, summer, winter, or fall? You probably have your favorite, but each has its own particular importance in the grand scheme of life. Each is different but complementary to the others.

I think you get the point that I'm illustrating here. People are like this also. If everyone thought and felt the same way, the world wouldn't work like it does now. I have to believe that there is a reason for our differences, and I think that one day, we will all see that we are complementary, not just conflicting. I hope this book will help some of us move in that direction.

Our World of Duality

It has been said that there are two ends to every stick and that we can't truly know what something is without its opposite to compare it to. This is what is known as duality. So you wouldn't know what is good without something bad to contrast it with. There would be no comprehension of hard without soft, up without down, in without out, sweet without sour, or black without white. And so it goes for male and female. How about liberal and conservative? Play this game with everything you see in your world, and it will open your eyes to this duality thing we have going on here.

> Without contraries is no progression. Attraction and repulsion, reason
> and energy, love and hate, are necessary to human existence.
> —William Blake, *The Marriage of Heaven and Hell*

Most of us probably haven't really thought about the idea of duality. It is a simple concept that is also quite profound. It has been around for thousands of years as an ancient and revered Oriental philosophy called the *Tao,* which helped explain duality and how it permeates everything in our lives. Taoism is also a religion based upon the philosophy that began in China more than 2,500 years ago.

The *Tao* developed the yin-yang principle to characterize and illustrate the conflicting, yet complementary polarity that can be observed in everything. Lao Tzu expressed the Taoist principles in the *Tao Te Ching,* which is one of the world's oldest and most translated works. Here is a translated verse from the *Tao Te Ching* by J. H. McDonald (1996).

When people see things as beautiful, ugliness is created.
When people see things as good, evil is created.
Being and non-being produce each other.
Difficult and easy complement each other.
Long and short define each other.
High and low oppose each other.
Fore and aft follow each other.

The cosmos is built on this duality.

Duality exists at all levels in our day-to-day life experiences—down to the very atomic particles that create our world. This particular duality has had scientists searching to understand its importance since the 1920s when the wave-particle duality theory was presented. This was integral to the development of quantum mechanics. Physicists found that all photons, electrons, neutrons, protons, subatomic particles, atoms, and molecules are constantly flip-flopping between a solid particle state and an invisible wave state.

This means that all solid matter as we know it, feel it, see it, and sense it is constantly appearing, disappearing, materializing, and dematerializing, but we are unable to see it happen because it does it so fast or in a way that our senses can't acknowledge. I'm not making this up!

Margaret Wertheim, a well-known physicist, sums up this duality in quantum physics:

> In the quantum world, subatomic particles lurch about, suddenly disappearing from their starting points and reappearing as if by magic somewhere else. … In many cases you cannot watch a subatomic particle move from A to B; you can only observe it at point A, and, sometime later, observe it again at point B. Just how it got there is a mystery. In this realm particles sometimes act entirely like waves, and vice versa. This equivalence of particles and waves is related to the equivalence of matter and energy that Einstein discovered. … How could nature be both things at once? How could both pictures be right? Yet how could either be wrong?
> —Margaret Wertheim, *Pythagoras' Trousers*

Our solid physical world is what we know to be our reality. Research questions this perception and invalidates it. Quantum physics is showing us glimpses of a nonphysical world that we are unable to see with our five senses. But just because we can't see something doesn't mean it isn't there.

Richard Conn Henry, professor of physics and astronomy at Johns Hopkins has a few words of wisdom for us in his article, "The Mental Universe." He said, "Get over it and accept the inarguable conclusion. The universe is immaterial, mental and spiritual!" He is saying that our physical world isn't really physical at all.

Duality states that we can't fully understand something without comparing and contrasting it to its opposite. I take that to mean that we can't really comprehend this physical world fully because we presently don't have the capability to recognize the nonphysical world that physicists have discovered coexisting right alongside of us.

There are many dualities in this world that most of us don't recognize for many reasons. This wave-particle duality is one we can all agree that we don't understand. How many other dualities are we unaware of? Throughout this book, we will be using the principle of duality for clarification of human nature.

Thoughts on the Brain

Perhaps the most significant duality for any of us lies within our brains. You may be already aware that your physical brain is divided into two distinct parts. According to some, the left side of the brain is primarily concerned with thinking and reasoning, and the right side of the brain is the emotional and feeling side.

The human brain is so complicated and complex that it is really an oversimplification to claim that it works in such a cut-and-dried fashion. This right brain-left brain theory does have merit as it describes for us the dual nature of human perception. It will be used here as a way to compare our disparities.

This split brain situation offers the possibilities of opposing perspectives, depending which side is in control, mostly in the realm of thinking and feeling. One main point that needs to be made here is that neither side is superior to the other. They just have different functions. Both are necessary to function fully as a human being. In fact, studies of head injuries have shown that serious, specific impairments occur with damage to one side or the other.

If your brain's hemispheres were separated and disconnected, certain things have been proven to happen. You can talk and think from the left side, but you couldn't recognize faces properly. The strange thing is that you wouldn't know that you couldn't. It wouldn't appear to be a problem because it would be a fundamental change in your conscious awareness.

Even though we need both sides of our brains, one side is predominating in almost all of us. If you didn't already know it, most men are left-brain oriented while most women are right-brain oriented. Of course, that leads to big-time complications that will be discussed in the chapters ahead. Although typical, not all men and women fit this stereotype.

Here are some of the functions of the different sides of the brain:

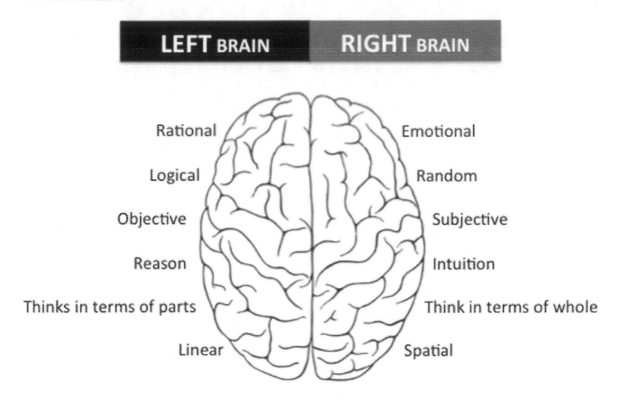

I am very left brained while my wife is very right brained. Do the math. When we attempt to communicate from our respective sides of our brains, more times than not, we enter into a conflicting and adversarial situation. I have learned that if I am going to be effective with her, I have to concentrate on trying to speak her language. Men and women sometimes really speak different languages, and a good part of it is because of how their brains functions.

The human brain is a fascinating subject and emphasizes again what a key role dualities play in the lives of each and every one of us. As you will find as you read on, there are many mysteries of human behavior that can be linked to how our brains function.

A study done by Diamond and Hopson (1998) finds that the human brain has as many as one hundred billion neurons with a trillion supporting cells, called the glia. Together, the nerve cells make up an estimated quadrillion synaptic connections within it. Scientists and researchers are just beginning to understand how our behaviors and our physical brains are related.

Since the brain is so complex and transcends our present understanding, it should be taken for granted that new research may invalidate our present-day interpretations. New information will continue to uncover some of its mysteries and help us better understand ourselves.

A Great Observation Still Little Understood

And this leads us to the great observation made by a number of brilliant minds before us, which is still almost unknown and little understood. That is, in addition to gender, there are dualities in temperament. These dualities are based on opposite traits that compete with each other in their inherent values. The basis for most of our conflicts is rooted here.

Science is beginning to accumulate data that is showing that people may be born with certain temperaments and personality traits according to genetic makeup. We may be similar to our parents, but we often are different in many ways. The whole process has almost a magical quality. It is becoming apparent that each of us has a basic temperament programmed at birth, and like the seasons, it is there for a reason. From there, each of us has traits that make us who we are and make us special in the makeup of society and the world in general.

The key, of course, is to know ourselves and where we fit in—in order to become comfortable with whom we are. And we can begin to understand others in order to appreciate them and their value to the big picture. This is fascinating and extremely enlightening, and it allows us to put conflicts in a less personal arena. And from that, comes peace in the valley.

If all of this seems like it is too good to be true, it is anything but. It is factual, and it can be learned in a relatively short time. The results can be spectacular for individuals, family members, local communities, nations, and the world.

I believe that learning the basics of the dualities of human nature and recognizing how they create conflicts in our world is critical to solving the problems we face. As you read on, this will become more easily understood.

One problem is clear. Our inability to get along with each other seems to be on the rise. Once again, just look at the divorce rate. Take a look at the turmoil in the world. Something isn't working the way we are going at it. Maybe understanding our duality will begin to help us find some solutions.

In order to begin to appreciate the duality aspects of our world, I have written this summary poem with the sole purpose of uncovering it. Enjoy!

This world is made of contrasts
Black versus white

Opposites in nature
It's wrong or it's right

The logic of our emotions
Joy turns to sorrow

Some die for today
The rest live for tomorrow

Blooming prosperity
Becomes a barren existence

We give up and lose
Or win with persistence

Infinity is eternal
But youth turns to old

Mind over matter
Hot embers grow cold

Which path will we choose
There's no way to tell

'Cause this could be heaven
Or this could be our hell

Lesson 2

I Hate People Like That

*Hatred is blind, anger is foolhardy, and he who pours out
vengeance risks having to drink a bitter draught.*
—Alexandre Dumas, *The Count of Monte Cristo*

Think about this for a moment and be honest: Aren't there certain types of people you naturally dislike? For some of us, it's people who are insensitive and rude. For others, it's people who talk too much. Some hate it when people won't talk and are uncommunicative—and how about wishy-washy people who can't make decisions on their own?

You can add to that short list a number of reasons why we don't like people who are different from us. How about people who don't look like us or act like us? What about people who don't have the same values as we do? I'm not just talking about differences in race and religion, even though this has been an obvious problem universally throughout history.

Being with people who are different from us can be difficult and uncomfortable. And because of this, it can be natural to rationalize that these people aren't up to our standards and may even be inferior to us. It allows us to believe we are better than they are. And it becomes very easy to make the decision to "hate people like that."

Why do we feel this way? Where do these judgments come from? Is it a conscious decision we make? Do we have a choice in the matter? Do our reactions just come to us naturally? Actually, these are examples of the natural conflicts that are built into each and every one of us. This is the stuff the world is built around: people being in conflict with people who are not the same as they are. It's a major component of human nature.

One reason this is a problem is that these people generally invalidate who we are by being opposed to the things we hold dear. Each of us is born to think and feel in ways that are different from others. This all seems in accordance with a natural balance in the world. Each of us has a keen sense of self that leads us to believe that our way of perceiving and judging is totally right and justified. And so it follows that those who don't see it our way have to be wrong.

Why else would there be so much conflict between people? We all see the world differently, and so much of this perspective is being shown to be genetically determined. We have opposite and competing views built in to the human condition. It is difficult to change our predetermined core preferences, and these preferences help shape the way we see the world around us.

If you think you are responsible for thoughtfully choosing all your preferences, try to change your preference in any significant choice you make. Try making yourself like something that you really don't like. Try making yourself dislike something you don't. If you can't do these things, then how can we expect others to do them?

What is the source of all your choices? And when you do make a choice, aren't you usually just doing what you already think or feel is right? If this is too hard to deal with now, just set the idea aside and revisit it after you have read further into the book. It won't seem as crazy as it may seem now.

The Conflict of Opposites

After I was married, it became increasingly clear to me just how different my wife and I were from each other. I was partnered with my complete opposite. Everything each of us wanted was in direct opposition to what the other wanted. Everything became a conflict of "my way" versus "her way." And I always ended up holding the short end of the stick.

Even if I happened to win and get my way, which was once in a blue moon, I always lost in the long run. For a person like me with a well-developed ego, this was more than a humbling experience. It was actually frightening!

> I could say day and you'd say night
> Tell me it's black when I know that it's white,
> It's always the same,
> It's just a shame, that's all.
> —Genesis, *That's All*

What do you do when you are in conflict with someone? We both loved each other very much, but we could sure push each other's buttons. Even when I bit my tongue and didn't say what was on my mind, she knew what I was thinking. She could actually feel what I was thinking. I knew then that I was in big trouble. There was no escaping this situation.

After going through what seemed like an eternity of marital emotional upsets due to our opposing ways, I was beginning to figure out that this conflict with my wife wasn't going away. No amount of force was going to change her, and I was tired of trying and always failing.

I came to the conclusion that if my marriage was going to work, I would have to give up some of my old self (ego) and relearn an awful lot in a short period of time. The analogy of a boot camp comes to mind. Isn't that what boot camp is all about—tearing down the old and replacing it with the new? The problem with this particular boot camp was that I didn't know I had signed up for it.

As it turned out, living with my direct opposite was truly a blessing in disguise because it opened my mind (and my heart) to new ways of thinking and understanding. Once again though, it was anything but easy. In his 1933 book, *Modern Man in Search of a Soul*, Carl Jung said, "The meeting of two personalities is like the contact of two chemical substances: if there is any reaction, both are transformed." That is exactly what happened to me!

It is said opposites attract. And that is true for my wife and me. It's true for a lot of couples I know, but it isn't true for everyone. Maybe nature forces this "opposites attract" thing for a reason we have yet to figure out. Perhaps it's to enable some of us to appreciate the worth of those unlike ourselves. Maybe it's all just a cruel hoax!

Whatever it is, we are missing the point of this opposites thing if more than one out of two marriages ends in divorce. Somewhere along the line, we began thinking that not having everything in common was grounds for separation.

How about the workplace? It bears a striking similarity to a marriage, and making it even more binding is the fact you spend so much time there. Aren't there people at work who constantly annoy you and are always butting heads with you?

How much productivity is lost in any organization because of disharmony due to personal conflicts? Although it is impossible to precisely answer this question, interpersonal conflicts have to be one of the most significant problems that interfere with a business running smoothly and efficiently. I have watched it happen in my own office with devastating effects.

The important thing is that we all learn from all this. It's not wishful thinking to realize these different types of people who annoy you can be just as valuable to an organization as you are—only in different ways. We will expand on this further in later lessons.

Birds of a Feather Flock Together.

At the same time, aren't we naturally attracted to people who closely resemble ourselves in values, likes, and judgments? It's certainly true in friendships, with business associates, and sometimes in marriage. Many highly successful marriages are between men and women of similar temperaments, but it probably depends upon which temperaments we're talking about.

When I was growing up, just about all my good friends had temperaments somewhat similar to mine. At least, they were close enough to where there wasn't a lot of conflict. If there was conflict, it probably wasn't worth my time to be friends. Sounds rather shallow, doesn't it? It just felt right to be with certain people, and it felt uncomfortable to be with others.

I don't think I was much different from most people when it came to this. I never had any problems with my friends. It was always fun and easy to be with them, and we had a lot of great times.

Obviously, the problem is not between those who are similar in temperament and other ways; it is with those who are different. Take the classic example of men and women themselves. Remember that most women are right brained (the feeling and intuitive side) and men are left brained (the logical and rational side). Now you know the source of what they call the "battle of the sexes."

When my wife and I are with other couples, it's amusing to see how the men eventually congregate in one area and the women in another. For the men, the conversation invariably turns to how we are amazed at what our wives do. We just can't understand how they think like they do and get away with it. Where is their reasoning process? It drives us crazy. It seems like we can't please them no matter what we do.

> Women have many faults,
> Men have only two:
> Everything they say,
> And everything they do.
> —Anonymous

I hear afterward from my wife that their conversation was largely concerned with how husbands don't show enough attention or affection—or aren't much fun to be around. Or we work too much and don't spend enough time with them.

Conclusion: Most women want their men to be more feeling toward them (more right-brained.) Most men want their women to think more like they do (more left-brained.)

We See it Happen Around the World.

Across the board and everywhere around the world, our differences define us. Truly, one of the most difficult tasks for all of us is to understand and accept different cultures. We aren't comfortable with what we don't understand, so we can become leery of it—and leery of them. We believe that they have to be really strange to live that way. This way of thinking, in turn, breeds fear and mistrust.

If there is an infraction by one side or both, this can escalate into violence of unparalleled proportions. Anger and hatred take over. All sorts of atrocities occur, and they all become self-justifiable because it's in retaliation for the wrongdoings of the other side.

This is why it is so important to learn from our mistakes and try to find ways to understand each other—rather than looking for better ways to destroy one another. The escalation of hate has no ending until it destroys one side or both. With the weapons of today, that is a real possibility.

We are told that it's in our nature to choose sides. It's a competitive world, after all. Examples of our sides can be: your country versus their country, your religion versus their religion, your political view versus their political view, your culture versus their culture, and, ultimately, your way versus their way.

And this even spills over into a national obsession for many of us; sports are an example that is clearly recognizable. Your team versus their team. If you're a sports fan (from the word fanatic), you know exactly what I'm talking about. If there is a team sport you follow, there is a rival team that really gets you riled up. It's very hard to feel kindly to anyone wearing that team's T-shirt. Maybe you don't truly hate him, but in the right circumstances, there might be an exchange of some words, or worse.

To people who aren't interested in sports, this kind of emotion just for a game seems ridiculous. And it is, of course—but not for a real fan.

Sometimes this competitive thing actually cascades into violence, riots, or death. It has happened before, and it will happen again. How can someone become so consumed with his or her team winning a game that he or she will risk physical harm or going to jail? The fact is that our veneer of civilization can be quickly cast off in the heat of the moment.

But it is not only sports rivalries that consume our emotions. How much time and energy is spent on other silly competitions just to be able to prove that someone or something is better than someone or something else? This also applies to our ideologies and our attachments to them.

I was taught that you never talk to people about politics and religion. The reason for that, of course, is that it is the best way to get into an argument with them and create hard feelings.

Politics has always been the source of much conflict and divisiveness because it is the fight for power of different viewpoints and values. It is one of the most evident examples of how humans fight each other to get their way.

And how many people have been killed throughout history when religions have clashed over who is right and who is wrong about their interpretation of God? It never ceases to amaze me how people can keep rationalizing doing this.

A Quick Look at Hate

I hate to have to talk about this subject, but hate is undoubtedly one of the major driving forces in this world. Just look at all the results of hate in our world. Violence, crimes, and wars fill our news reports every day. We can't possibly overlook how it affects every single one of us.

The duality of love and hate is at the top of the human experience. We will explore this uniquely human duality in some detail throughout this book. Hate is the problem; love is the solution. Let's start with what hate is and where it comes from. We need to work on understanding hate better so we can gain better control over it. Later in the book, we will focus on love.

Merriam-Webster's definition of hate is "an intense, extreme hostility and aversion to someone or something usually stemming from fear, anger, or a sense of injury." Hatred is often associated with feelings of anger and a disposition toward hostility. Hate is sourced from fear, which is one of the basic human emotions. Fear is the real issue behind hate.

Aristotle was one of the first to define hate for us back in the fourth century BC. He said that hate is a dislike for someone based on a negative perception of that person's nature that is so intense that whoever feels it wants to cause real harm to another. He also said that a person could hate another person or a whole group of people bearing the same stain.

The word *hate* is used very loosely and sometimes casually in our culture. One can say that they hate to exercise or they hate to eat broccoli. This kind of hate is obviously said without any real malice.

On the other hand, one can say that they hate someone who broke up their marriage or hurt their child or any number of violations that evoke extreme emotions. This results in the desire and justification for possibly retaliating in some way.

We may never let go of this kind of deep-seated hatred throughout our lives. We might even pass on this hate to future generations. Emotions like this have a huge impact on our humanly experiences in this world.

> I think that hate is a feeling that can exist where there is no understanding.
> —Tennessee Williams, *Sweet Bird of Youth*

We will try to create more understanding of human nature and hopefully make an impact on reducing some of the hate in the world. Being that hate is a byproduct of fear, we must explore its emotional sources. Emotions are so much a part of human nature that I'd be remiss to not discuss them in detail. An analysis of this human element will help us to understand ourselves, others, and why we all do what we do.

The Science of Emotions

The next few pages will be an investigation of how our emotions are hardwired into our brains. This will help us to understand how our emotions and feelings work. Emotions have always been a mystery to me, especially when they are negative and directed at me!

In *The Emotional Brain*, Joseph E. LaDoux, a leading authority in the field of neural science, explores the underlying brain mechanisms responsible for our emotions. He presents some pretty interesting findings about our emotions and how the brain is set up in a way that makes our emotional responses, including hate and fear, seem almost instinctual by nature.

For example, most of our capabilities to know danger and fear are present in infants before they have had an experience of that kind. He points out those emotional responses are prewired into the brain's circuitry. This means that emotions aren't learned, just evoked. As we go through life, the things that evoke our emotions as individuals are exposed and then labeled through our experiences.

In *The Emotional Brain*, LaDoux investigates what happens in our brains to make us feel emotions such as love, fear, and anger. His research sheds light on how these emotions control us. He says that once an emotion is turned on, it is difficult for the rational part of our brains to turn it off.

The neural connections from the source of these emotions are stronger and more developed than the connections from our rational brain back down. This implies that humans are hard-wired to be emotional beings more than rational beings. I think we will all agree on that!

Scientists have done extensive research on this subject, and they have developed some interesting theories on the basic, universal emotions that control just about everything we do. Not only are our emotions prewired genetically in our brains, they also are in control of our decision-making processes. Think of the implications this has on everyone's lives!

Antonio Damasio, a neuroscientist/neurobiologist, has made significant contributions to our understanding of emotions, feelings, decision making, and consciousness. He has devoted more than thirty years of research in this field and has written many important books on the subject. He is a professor at the University of Southern California, and he heads the Brain and Creativity Institute.

Damasio says that our emotions are tied into our value systems as the brain elicits hormones and neurotransmitters that create physical sensations that make us feel these emotions. Each emotion may have a certain physiological response because of the hormones and neurotransmitters. Emotions are how and why we perceive value. This is based upon how these brain chemicals make us feel. He also says that emotions play a central role in our decision-making process because of this brain-chemical-feeling relationship. There is very little choice in this process. This is sometimes nothing more than a stimulus-response scenario.

If all our decisions are based upon emotions, then learning about human nature must include an in-depth understanding of human emotion. I have to admit that for most of my life I was ignorant about how important emotions are to all of us. I think I spent most of my life trying to hide them, not trying to understand them. They sure seem to affect us on every level of our being.

Paul Ekman is an American psychologist who has researched different aspects of emotion for more than forty years. He is well known for his findings of the six basic emotions that are universal to all human beings. His research concluded that anger, surprise, fear, happiness, sadness, and disgust are innate to all of us. These emotions are present in all humans regardless of race, color, creed, and levels of literacy. This important concept helps us understand our humanness.

I have to conclude that if all of us are born with these specific emotions already embedded into our consciousness, then there is a distinct possibility that there could be many, many more inherent emotions that help create the individual temperaments that we all have. Paul Ekman's research helps to support the idea that our emotions are not learned but innate and programmed within us. Maybe all our preferences, likes, and dislikes—as well as the source of all our conflicts—have this innateness.

As I was pondering this emotional aspect of our lives, I needed to figure out the difference between an emotion and a feeling. After much processing I came to this conclusion. Our emotions are innate, and our feelings are personalized through our life processes. This means that we have the emotions from birth that control how we react to events. Most of these emotions are animal-like in nature and are there for our survival. Our feelings are formed when we have an emotion, and then we interpret the cause of its expression placing the blame on whatever stimulated the emotion. So our emotions come first, and then our interpretations of our emotions which then create our feelings. Our emotions are more physical in nature, and our feelings are psychological.

One thing is clear about human nature: we are very much controlled by our emotions and feelings. Understanding them is one of the keys to understanding ourselves and others. We will try to build upon work like this for our understanding of human nature. It is important to learn about these things in order to master the mystery of human nature. Hopefully, after gaining insights that will be discussed in this book, you won't be so prone to say, "I hate people like that."

As you read further, hang in there and open your mind to the magic of how different types of temperaments conflict with one another. It begins with understanding yourself first and then those who are different from you. You will see where everyone fits and why it's important to have all kinds. Hopefully, this can help resolve our conflicts and create a happier and more peaceful world, community, family, and you.

As the French say, "Viva la difference!"

Have some fun with the next summary poem! It will become obvious that this one is tongue-in-cheek.

I hate people like that (they all drive me crazy)
How can they do that, so dumb, lame, and lazy?

I've got a solution; it's the only one that works.
Make me the leader; I'll get rid of the jerks!

There wouldn't be a problem if everyone were like me.
We'd all get along, we'd all surely agree.

The world would be perfect if I could make this deal.
It all would go smoothly with me at the wheel.

With me in charge, they would have to say,
He knows how to do things the very best way.

But I guess this won't happen; I can't change the masses,
So I better learn how to put up with these asses.

Lesson 3

Four Seasons of Humanity (Our First Two Dualities)

Temperament: The manner of thinking, behaving, and reacting
characteristic of a specific individual; disposition.
—*The American Heritage Dictionary*

If we are going to understand human nature, we must recognize the differences that create the big picture of humanity. Temperaments have been one way to classify the different types of people in the world. Throughout the ages, philosophers and scientists have noted and written about the different temperaments of people. Generally, they have been broken down into four basic types with predictable characteristics that distinguish them from each other. It seems human nature mimics Mother Nature's four seasons. I'll show you how at the end of this lesson.

For some strange reason, this invaluable information has not become accessible to the general public. It is used in a minor way by businesses to help their salespeople better understand their customers in order to increase sales. Some high school counselors use profiling to help students find their niches in the world. Beyond that, most of this knowledge has been communicated among scientists, academics, and a small number of others.

My goal is to simplify this information without diluting it, make it easily understood by virtually anyone, and lead to a better understanding and appreciation for people who are different from you and me. This all begins with understanding the main dualities that shape us all. From there, we can begin to get a basic understanding of human nature.

The First Two Dualities (and You're One of Them)

The easiest way to begin our exploration into the four basic temperaments is to go back to the concept of duality. There are two dualities that create the basic types that define us all. No one is exempt.

The first duality is based on the two opposing ways we experience the world as human beings.

We can experience life primarily with our heads (objectively with our thinking) or primarily with our hearts (subjectively with our feelings).

Of course, we all do both to some degree, but one will dominate for each of us. Our first duality is thinking versus feeling. Logically enough, people who use thinking as their dominant way of experience we will call thinkers. Conversely, those who use feelings as their dominant way we will call feelers.

This duality is first and foremost in shaping and affecting our lives. You see, nature has pulled a fast one on us. As it was explained before, the majority of men are thinkers (left brain), and the majority of women are feelers (right brain). Researchers claim it's a two-thirds majority for both. Herein is the cause of much of the differences between the sexes. And who is not affected by this?

And here's the second!

The second duality is how we go about processing information. It starts by where our attention is focused—either inside ourselves where we interpret life through concepts and principles or by reacting immediately to what is happening outside us to people and things.

People who are internally focused tend to take life to a deeper level by seeking underlying meaning to events in their lives. Conversely, people who are externally focused are much more aware and sensitive to their environments. Each is a totally opposite way to view the world. For people who are externally focused, the way they think and feel is strongly influenced by what is going on around them at the moment. The world acts upon them in a literal way. We will call people who are like these outers.

For the opposite kind of people who are internally focused, we call them inners. They process their life experiences through a deeply held set of inner concepts and principles that allows for an interpretation of what's going on. Have you noticed how some people are quick to act when something happens (outers) while others take their time to make decisions (inners)? Outers will generally act first and then feel or think. Inners have a natural tendency to feel or think first and then act.

Putting the Two Dualities Together

Our basic temperament is formed by a combination of these two dualities. Combining the two dualities results in the four human seasons—the four basic temperaments. So we can be either a feeler or a thinker and at the same time be either an outer or inner. This gives us four possible temperament combinations or four kinds of people: (1) inner feelers, (2) outer feelers, (3) inner thinkers, and (4) outer thinkers.

Here it is in chart form:

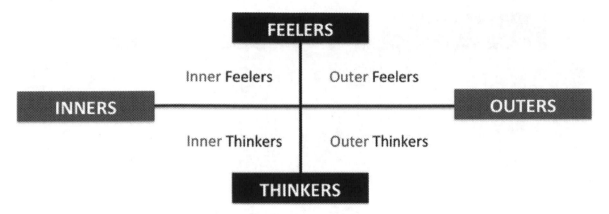

Which one are you? How about the people who are close to you? Here are some words to help you identify each of the dualities.

THINKERS	VS.	**FEELERS**
Objective		Subjective
Policy		Society
Laws		Circumstances
Firmness		Persuasion
Impersonal		Personal
Standards		Good or bad
Critique		Appreciate
Analyze		Sympathetic
Practicality		Beauty

INNERS	VS.	**OUTERS**
Private		Interactive
Depth		Breadth
Intensive		Extensive
Conserve		Expand
Internal Processing		External reactions
Principles		People
Concepts		Things
Fewer, deeper relationships		Many casual friendships

Immediately after our "I dos" were exchanged, I had to take a crash course in Feelings 101. My wife seemed to have more feelings in her little finger than I had in my whole being. I always prided myself on being a person of reason, logic, and intellect. It had served me pretty well—getting me through college and dental school and helping me become a better dentist technically. I was fairly well read and usually had decent common sense. But all this amounted to little compared to the power and intensity of my bride's feelings, especially if I had unknowingly hurt them. Wow!

Then it hit me. If I was creating such explosive feelings in her, then what I was doing to others similar to her might be creating a similar response. Others in my world might perceive me as she did. Not good.

My on-the-job training and learning about feelings was similar to a dog surrounded by a moving, invisible electric fence. Every time I crossed that emotional line, I got zapped. Trouble was, I didn't know exactly where the fence was located. But I began to learn. I got better. I'm still learning.

Feelers are by nature mostly concerned with people and what is happening to them. They have empathy and respond well to the needs of others. Their emotions (both good and bad) are tuned in to the people around them. Relationships are their number one priority. They can cry readily viewing emotional movies or at least get choked up. But like the moving invisible electric fence, their feelings can change abruptly and unexpectedly.

Thinkers, on the other hand, are more in tune to the task at hand and getting the job done. Their interests lie mostly in the physical world. Because thinking has a certain logic and reasoning to it (even if it's incorrect), thinkers are more predictable than feelers.

Where Would the World be Without People Like You?

Which is better—a feeler or a thinker? If you're a feeler, you'd no doubt vote for your team. But just look around you at all those conveniences and technical advancements you love—from dishwashers to airplanes. All the advancements in medicine, science, transportation, construction, computers, electronics, energy, etc. were the product of thinkers.

If you're a thinker, you're probably convinced your side is better. But where would the world be without beauty, compassion, sympathy, love, music, literature, poetry, sports, humor, theater, movies, all the arts, and all the things that some people believe make life worth living? With all of our advancements in science and technology, are we any closer to individual happiness and peace in the world?

My wife and I recently built our dream home. I drew up the floor plans and designed all the architectural features of the house. She couldn't read a blueprint if she had to, but she picked out everything else—colors, carpet and flooring, light fixtures, landscaping, trim, and anything to do with interior and exterior decorating. I'm slightly colorblind and wouldn't have attempted what she did. Together, I believe we created a masterpiece we can be proud of. Not a bad example of what we're talking about—a feeler and a thinker complementing each other. There's an old saying—men make houses, and women make homes.

Are You an Outer or an Inner?

Are you an outer (stimulated more by external conditions) or an inner (an internally focused person)? By the way, most temperament profilers have used the terms extroverts and introverts. But there is a negative connotation about being an introvert that isn't always warranted. Using their descriptions, it makes sense to make the real duality the way people are normally focused.

Outers act quickly, spontaneously, and decisively. They can do this because there is little or no internal processing that has to be done. Inners are slower to act, but they can be a little less reactive because their words or actions have been clarified by internal beliefs or values.

Debra Johnson, a research scientist in psychology at the University of Iowa, has shown that introverts and extroverts (inners and outers) have different brain activity. She published a study (*American Journal of Psychiatry*, February 1999) that was the first to reveal this connection of temperament and how the brain works. There is a part of the brain called the thalamus (actually there is a pair of them) that is important to our capabilities of awareness. It is like a switchboard for information that we process.

There is so much information in the world to be aware of that we would be overwhelmed with trying to be aware of everything all at once. The thalamus is in charge of allowing only so much information through at a time. Inners predominately use the front part of the thalamus that is responsible for remembering, planning, and processing ideas. Outers use the back part of the thalamus, which is responsible for experiencing outside sources of stimulation.

My wife is quick to act when stimulated externally. She's great in social functions because of her quick wit. She thinks on her feet and can usually persuade almost anyone to do anything. It's quite a talent. I, on the other hand, can write a book and work with people in a calm and deliberate manner. I'm not very comfortable in social situations, and she doesn't excel in non-stimulating situations.

Inners, like me, are good listeners because they have the capacity to process and understand what others are saying and hopefully find the underlying meaning of what is being said. Outers, like my wife, tend to get impatient or hung up on the literal meaning of the words. Listening may not be their forte.

Result: two dualities working together at the same time with each having the same 50 percent distribution within the population. This gives us four combinations of temperaments that have been described by philosophers for eons. In fact, learned observers of the human scene from many cultures have talked about these four different temperaments for centuries. They have labeled them in a number of ways, but in essence, their descriptions mirror mine.

For ease and clarity, I will use the Merrill-Reid Social Styles classifications—the amiables, expressives, analyticals, and drivers—for our basic temperament model. This model has been used extensively since their book, *Personal Styles and Effective Performance,* was published in 1984. The classification names are easy to remember and they also describe each basic temperament to a T. Let's look briefly at each. This information is presented only as an introduction since many books have been written on this subject. Try to figure out which temperament describes you the best.

Inner Feelers—Amiables

They have a deep set of core feelings that help them relate to people in very empathetic ways. With the ability to process and understand the feelings of their fellow humans, they are excellent at helping others and can form deep relationships. They're friendly and easy to get along with. People have the most value for them, and they are labeled as amiables.

Inner Thinkers—Analyticals

These people have a deep set of core principles and use logic, intellect, and analysis to direct and guide them through their lives. They usually excel in matters of the physical world and are often good at complex and tedious tasks. Logically enough, they are called analyticals.

Outer Feelers—Expressives

Here are people who love stimulation and excitement. They're easy to recognize because they usually talk a lot. Loving to be in the forefront of everything they do, they are adept at motivating and directing others. These are the expressives.

Outer Thinkers—Drivers

They want to control events with will and determination. These people get the job done and are very concerned with how well, how fast, and how efficiently it is accomplished. They're usually excellent in business and anything to do with productivity and profit. Meet the drivers.

Again, which one are you? The following page gives explicit descriptions of each type to help you determine which you are. How these temperaments—and you—fit into the big picture will come in the pages ahead.

This next chart will give greater meaning to you by being able to see the opposing values of the temperaments on one page. Compare and contrast the opposing temperaments alongside each other to better understand their differences. Try to find yourself—and other significant people in your life—here. We are going to start calling our temperament descriptions, charts, and their significance the "T-Code" for simplicity's sake. The "T" is for temperament.

There is more to understanding ourselves and others than what will be presented with this chart. But it is a great place to begin our discovery of the secrets of human nature.

We need to understand the roots of all the conflict we experience in this world. In order to do this, we have to begin to understand the importance of each of the temperament types in the big picture. This will begin the process of building more tolerance and compassion for those who are different than us. Hopefully, we will begin to see that we are complementary with our opposites and realize our conflicts don't have to be so divisive.

Here is our first T-Code chart of the four basic temperaments.

FEELERS

Amiables (Close Relationships)
"Does it help someone?"

Altruistic
Great relationship builders
Strong team members
Good listeners
Slow to act
Adverse to conflict
Desire the opinions of others
Adverse to risk
Indirect in speech
Low assertiveness
Highly responsive
Casual, stylish
Liberal arts, communications or non-
   technical business degree

Expressives (High Energy Interactions)
"How does it make me feel?"

Hedonistic
Good relationship builders
Strong presenters & persuaders
Confident
Poor focus on details
Defensive when challenged
Unfocused listeners
Quick decisions, spontaneous
Easy to be with
Tend to change their minds, flexible
Get sidetracked easily
Somewhat disorganized
High responsiveness
High assertiveness

INNERS   **OUTERS**

Analyticals (Factual & Logical)
"Does it make sense?"

Stoic
Organized
Handle complexity well
Fail to connect with people
Deliberate
Inflexible
Interactions can be dull
Formal, conservative
Good listeners
Low responsiveness
Low assertiveness
Technical background or degree

Drivers (Task Oriented)
"Does it work – is it productive?"

Pragmatic
Organized
Action oriented, high assertiveness
Inflexible, sometimes arrogant
Impatient listeners, low responsiveness
Quick decisions
Their way or the highway
High stress interactions
Bottom line most important
Direct in speech
Task focused
Technical or business degree

THINKERS

When you look at this chart, try to notice which groups are in opposition to each other. It's obvious that the expressives are opposites of the analyticals. Also the amiables are opposites of the drivers. Try to apply this source of conflict in your life—either directly or with the people around you.

Can you see that there are some similarities to these groups based upon the proximity in the chart? So the amiables share some characteristics with the analytical and the expressives, but not the drivers. The drivers share some of the characteristics of the analyticals and the expressives, but not the amiables. This allows us to begin to understand some of the ways we are naturally more comfortable with some temperaments than others.

This chart shows the basic four temperament types. There is much more to temperaments than this model, and we will go into more detail later in the book. This is a great beginning for us to start seeing the differences in temperaments and how they can conflict with another.

Humanity is shaped by the conflicting values of these four temperaments—just as our physical world is shaped by the conflicting nature of Mother Nature's seasons. Throughout this book, I attempt to show that all of our human thoughts, feelings, and actions are expressions of the values that are inherent to these four temperaments.

How do the four temperaments reflect Mother Nature's four seasons? I believe the basics can be understood in simple terms, yet it can also become a profound subject if pondered. In simple terms, I compare the traits and symbolic meanings of the seasons and the temperaments that correspond to them.

Spring

This is the beginning of the growing season of nature, a time of birth and nurturing the young. Caring, nurturing, and family are distinguishing values here. These are amiable traits.

Summer

A season to enjoy the good and prosperous times, socializing, vacations, and taking time for recreation. Having fun, being stimulated, and getting out. These are the values of the expressives.

Fall

This is the time for harvesting and reaping what has been sown. The rewards for all your labors come to fruition. Getting and stockpiling for the next season. Drivers can relate to this.

Winter

It is the season to come inside out of the cold. It is time to fix things and prepare for the next season. It is time for introspection, contemplation, and reflection. This is what the analytical does best.

The more I think about this, the more it all fits. This information helps me become closer to the physical world.

While sorting this material out in my head, a thought came to mind. As we become more dependent upon technology, we are getting further away from nature. Nature has become more of a backdrop than our connection to a higher power as it was in more "primitive" cultures. We seem so disconnected from it that we are missing out on the beauty, awe, and wonderment of the physical world, which we have been so very blessed with.

Understanding this model of opposite and competing values is imperative for being able to master the mystery of human nature.

Our next summary poem is about the lesson that is available to us between the similarities of the four seasons of humanity and nature. Life is very mysterious, but we have clues available that help us solve our problems. We need to look a little harder.

The four seasons of humanity,
Mother Nature's mirrored reflection.
All the magnificent parallels
Lay open for its inspection.

Hidden before our very eyes,
Our minds inept to this glory.
The mysteries that ever bewilder,
Our human nature is the story.

The seasons work in harmony,
Human differences create the strife.
All things complementary,
The purpose of this life.

If we could glimpse man's true potential,
Our conflicts would be less frightening.
The problems become opportunity,
With society's newfound enlightening.

Lesson 4

Uniting the Divided

True observers of nature, although they may think differently, will still agree that everything that is, everything that is observable as a phenomenon, can only exhibit itself in two ways. It is either a primal polarity that is able to unify, or it is a primal unity that is able to divide. The operation of nature consists of splitting the unified or uniting the divided; this is the external movement of systole and diastole of the heartbeat, the inhalation and exhalation of the world in which we live, act, and exist.
—Johann Wolfgang von Goethe, *Theory of Colors*

The magnificent parallels that can be found within human nature's temperaments and Mother Nature's seasons are profound—and absolutely imperative to our understanding of this amazing world. This knowledge will become the instructive foundation to help us recognize how the world really works. The importance of learning this is critical, and it holds the solutions to most of the human problems that are created by our duality-based conflicts.

I made mention in the last lesson that the four temperaments mimicked Mother Nature's four seasons. Each of our four seasons has special attributes and functions that can be paralleled by the human temperaments. Human nature has so much in common with Mother Nature, and it is important for us to see the similarities.

Let's start by saying that just as each of the seasons has their reasons for being, so do all the temperament types. So there is no ultimate basis for any judgment here, believing that one type is superior to the other. Our world couldn't work in any other way than it does now with the equal balance of the temperaments. I pointed out how the seasons are conflicting in nature but complementary as well. This concept is critical for learning its lessons.

A Model for Success

How does this relate to our real-world, everyday life? How can this knowledge benefit you? Understanding people is the cornerstone of being successful in your personal relationships and your career. If you could master these areas of your life, how much better could it get? Let's begin our mastery with becoming aware of the foundation of our humanity.

In order to really understand human nature, we need core explanations that are simple to understand and easy to communicate to others. This is something that has been sorely absent in the scientific community. There have been a multitude of books about trying to understand human nature, but for the most part, they are written in a language that most people can't or won't exert the massive energy and concentration it takes to get through the work. The KISS principle tells us to "keep it simple, stupid!" I will do my utmost to adhere to this philosophy.

Science demands that if a model is used to prove a theory, then it must be true in all circumstances. Models are made to simplify systems and help explain information. Mother Nature's model of opposite and competing—yet complementary—seasons yield so much of the knowledge and wisdom we need to gain an understanding of life. It sounds pretty simplistic. The big picture of humanity is built on the same model of opposites.

One of the major facets of human nature can be explained in the same way that Mother Nature can be explained. There are opposite and competing values that shape us as individuals, in our temperaments and in our behaviors. These conflicting values create the world in which we live. Just as summer and winter and spring and fall are opposites in nature, so can be our basic temperaments. These seasons are equal in their impact on the whole—as are the different temperaments.

Mother Nature's model can be found in most every aspect of the world, if we look close enough. My realization of this model came as I was doing some background reading for a research project. I was introduced to a model of business that made so much sense because it immediately and clearly helped me understand what was missing in my own business.

In academia-ville, much has been written by scholars trying to describe what is structurally critical for businesses or organizations to succeed, but this particular model, published by Robert Quinn, was basically identical to the model of the four basic temperament types (the T-Code). Called the *Competing Values Framework*, it covered four "domains" that Dr. Quinn described as being opposite and competing in their values. He said they were essential for success in any business or organization.

He believed that in order to be successful, a business has to be concerned with these opposite and competing values. I found that these domains reflected the qualities of the four temperaments and the four seasons.

His information was the impetus that started me on my quest to write this book. When I read his work, it hit me like a ton of bricks. It was more than just a business model; it was a model for everything humans are and do in this world. Thank you, Dr. Quinn, for enlightening me!

These opposite and competing domains represented the values that are characterized by the four temperaments. I saw the similarities between the seasons and our temperaments, but I also saw how necessary they all were for creating a business system that works—but only when they all are in balance and harmony.

Dr. Quinn explained in his *Competing Values Framework Model* that four domains have to work in unity if the business was to thrive. As I understood his model, I began to put the pieces of the puzzle together. I saw that his four domains were expressed by the four temperaments and their values. There is so much information that comes from his model but here is a simplification of it.

These competing domains are:

- Concern for people in the organization (team development, coaching, and supervision). This reminded me of the qualities of an amiable whose number one priority is people.
- Structure (roles and function, policies, replication, and procedures). This is definitely an Analytical characteristic.
- Production (goals, profitability and outcomes). Who is better than a driver at achieving?
- Innovation and change (flexibility, new and improved processes). An expressive likes stimulation and excitement.

These domains basically describe the strengths of the four temperaments and the qualities that they inherently have. Can you see that a business needs all types to succeed within this framework? Just like all the seasons are necessary to support life on earth.

By learning the different temperaments, you will also learn that the basic components of business have their roots in the different temperament's characteristics. For example, the amiable temperament is concerned mostly with people and taking care of people's needs.

In business, taking care of people is one of the most important components—so learning from the amiables is critical. Good relationships are mandatory for success in any business. As a consumer, don't you like friendly, helpful businesspeople? It all begins with an internal focus of supporting, nurturing, and growing the business's employees by improving morale. Happy employees mean happy customers!

And the opposite of the amiable is the driver who brings to the business table an opposing but equal component: being productive, effective, and profitable. There is nothing wrong with making money, but as everyone knows, it is not and should not be the only focus of business. On the other hand, a business will not and cannot survive for very long if it isn't profitable. Profitability can be best achieved when things are done right the first time. Drivers make things happen.

In any business, there are procedures, skills, methods, or activities that have to be done over and over again. In whatever field of endeavor, a business performs a service or produces a product, and that is the purpose of the business. In order to maximize the efficiency or effectiveness of these activities, the best way to do things is uncovered and then replication systems are created.

These activities are analyzed in order to do them in the right way time after time. Who is the best at analyzing? Who else but the analytical?

The opposite of the analytical is the expressive. What they value is stimulation, change, and the excitement of things that are new and improved. Everything in this world changes. Nothing stays the same. Change is a huge factor in what drives our commerce. This keeps untold numbers of people employed, creating new and improved ways of doing things. Expressives thrive in this flexible environment.

Bottom line: In any business, organization, or group, each basic temperament brings to the table an inherent strength that is absolutely necessary to succeed. Deficiency in any one is going to create a problem that makes success difficult or impossible.

All this information is being presented to make some specific points. One thing to grasp is that every temperament type has its worth in the grand scheme of life. We are all important to the workings of this world. Once we fully understand this, we might not be so judgmental with people who aren't like us, especially the ones who are opposite of us. The other thing to glean from all this is that business reflects how our model of life works. Unity of opposite values is a secret to success.

What Does it Take to be a Business Leader?

Robert Quinn also developed a leadership model based on the same structure of his *Competing Values Framework.* He said, "An effective leader has to be able to juggle opposite and competing values within the organization and be able to do it simultaneously."

Try to imagine keeping the status quo for maximum efficiency and then trying to change things to keep up with the times. Or try concentrating on your customers' needs and your employees' needs at the same time. Not easy.

But the effective leader has to do exactly that over and over again. In summary, an effective leader has to be able to do opposing tasks simultaneously.

1. Mentor and facilitate employees (amiable-like).
2. Coordinate the structure of the organization (analytical).
3. Be director of production (driver).
4. Be an innovator (expressive).

As you can see, this is just more of the same: utilizing the strengths of each of the four quadrants of the T-Code. In order to become effective, it appears that a leader has to adapt the qualities that are represented in all four seasons and our competing values model.

Can you recognize the fact that a leader has to step out of his/her basic temperament and not only learn but master the qualities of the other temperaments? That is difficult, and it's also very special and rare. A leader must be able to have an internal unity of these opposing values.

All of us have the opportunity to learn the qualities of the opposing temperaments in order to become more well–rounded people. No matter what you do or who you are, all of us can benefit from this information and become more effective in life. We don't have to be stuck in a rut just because of our temperaments.

We can extrapolate this business information and apply it to our personal effectiveness, success, and happiness. Much has been written and discussed about a balance in life that helps create positive outcomes for those who can juggle the different aspects of life. In order to have a balance, it is important to know what to balance. Our Mother Nature model once again is helpful.

The seasons—and our individual lives—the temperaments, the business model, and the leadership model all have competing and opposing values. Their attributes are in alignment with everything we have discussed so far. Quite simply, balance is making sure we don't sacrifice success in one aspect of our lives for another.

We will never be perfectly in balance because life is dynamic and always changing. As we get out of balance, life has a way of letting us know where we need to devote our attention and energy. Here are the opposing parts of life that I believe we all need to balance. Ask yourself how you are doing in each of these aspects of life:

- We all have the need and desire for good healthy relationships.
- Work is an environment where we can help others and create value to society.
- Adequate time devoted to recreation, which is a time to relax, enjoy, and recreate oneself.
- Setting personal goals to accomplish and achieve helps create a fruitful, productive life.

Work and play are obviously opposing aspects of life. Relationships are about dealing with others. Setting personal goals for growth and achievement are all about you. You can see how concentrating on one aspect can be contrary to the other. Happy juggling!

Philosophies of Human Nature

Over the thousands of years of recorded history, there have been a multitude of philosophers who have left their marks on our understanding of human nature. Familiar names such as Plato, Socrates, and Aristotle from ancient times, Francis Bacon, Rene Descartes, John Locke, David Hume, Fredrick Nietzsche, Sigmund Freud, and many more from more modern times have contributed to our accumulation of knowledge of human nature. For the most part, the study of philosophy is limited to intellectuals and academicians. Most of us probably don't have much of a working knowledge of these people's work. I know I don't.

Philosophy is the study of general and fundamental problems, such as those connected with reality, existence, knowledge, values, reason, mind, and language. Philosophy has a strong reliance on rational argument. The word philosophy comes from ancient Greece and literally means "love of wisdom."

Not everyone studies philosophy, but everyone has an internal core philosophy that allows him or her to perceive themselves, others, and the world in general. This creates the experience of life. It may be difficult for one to succinctly express their philosophy, but it shows in our behaviors, thoughts, and feelings. In other words, it shows in our natures. (Remember the definition of human nature?)

Each of us has a way of viewing the world that is influenced by a number of aspects of life, including genetic makeup. Philosophers have been arguing their different viewpoints about human nature for thousands of years. There are opposing philosophical theories about human nature that have established their "camps," and there is still debate about who is right and who is wrong.

Philosophers haven't used their enlightened knowledge to come to any common agreement yet. What good is all that knowledge if it doesn't help us common folk solve our problems? I believe that philosophers suffer from the same afflictions as other human beings. There are opposing and competing values in everyone's viewpoints, and philosophers are just as human in that regard as everyone else. Just because they are philosophers doesn't make them all see things the same way or have the same values.

It is only natural for us to see life through a unique lens. Our personal perception becomes our reality, and we can only see our own reality—not anyone else's. Metaphorically, when you are a hammer, everything you see looks like a nail. We see what we project from our own internal reality, and we all see things differently. A lot of it is based upon our inherent temperaments and values.

Once again, Mother Nature's competing values model holds the answer for us all. Let's look at the different camps of human nature philosophy and how they work with their competing values.

In Steven Pinker's 2002 best seller, *The Blank Slate*, he discusses these different groups of theories of human nature and their implications on us as individuals and society as a whole. Dr. Pinker is a world-renowned expert on language and the mind and is a professor of psychology at Harvard University. This book was a finalist for the Pulitzer Prize.

The main gist of his book was to dispel the widely accepted belief that human beings are born with a "blank slate" and that nurture is the dominant force in shaping us into being who we are. The blank slate is one of the main categories of philosophical thought that human nature theories can be subdivided into. Blank slate theorists believe that the mind is only shaped by our external experiences as we are born with no predisposed genetic influences.

John Locke (1631–1704) was the one of the first to maintain that we are born without innate ideas and that knowledge was determined from experience derived from sense perception. In other words, we are born as blank slates and become who we are from our experiences in our lives. Why is this important to know? His work still impacts us today in some very important ways. His thinking directly influenced some very important people—people like Thomas Jefferson, James Madison, Alexander Hamilton, and many more of our Founding Fathers.

In our Constitution, there are very important concepts that come directly from Locke's works. Life, liberty, equality, and the pursuit of happiness were attributed to him. Our form of government—whose power arises from the consent of its people—has roots in his philosophies. He also said that if the government infringes on these rights, then it needs to be changed.

Locke was also called the father of classical liberalism. His *Theory of the Mind* is often cited as the origin of the modern concept of the identity and the self. This philosophy has had a major effect on our educational system, our judicial laws in regard to personal rights, and even our ideas on parenting. So you can see the influence he has had on our lives.

The blank slate theory has some obvious flaws, especially with what science is uncovering recently about genetics, the brain and its functions. In his book, Pinker points out the social and political ramifications of its deficiencies and the dangers therein. If we adhere to only the blank slate philosophy of thought, we are missing out on the big picture. Pinker goes on to discuss the other groups of thought on human nature.

Pinker says that the second category of philosophical thought on human nature is called the ghost in the machine, which I say is the polar opposite of the blank slate. It proclaims that human nature is the internal functioning of the brain and is there from birth.

René Descartes (1596–1650) is said by many to be the father of modern Western philosophy. The ghost in the machine theory of human nature was highly influenced by his works. He took a very analytical approach in his work, beginning with the premise that only deductive and logical thought was real. He felt that our perception of the world was incorrect because our emotions obscured reality. He concluded that deductive reasoning was the only reliable method of obtaining knowledge. Sensory perceptions (feelings) come to us involuntarily and are not "willed" by us and therefore are inaccurate.

Descartes said, "I think, therefore I am." (Notice he doesn't say anything about feelings.) Our reality is shaped and guaranteed by our own self-consciousness. In *The Description of the Human Body,* he suggested that the body works like a machine and follows the laws of nature. He felt like the body had one nature, and our minds had another. Because of our consciousness, humans have free will, which directs choices and behaviors. This makes us responsible and accountable for all our deeds. He believed that there was an invisible essence residing in our brains that will continue on after death of the body. The mind is the arbiter of human destiny.

Descartes greatly influenced our culture. His methods of scientific deductions and heavy emphasis on mathematics led us in the way modern Western cultures go about solving many problems. By placing the body and mind into different realms, he directly influenced psychology, medicine, and science. By separating technology (physical) from ethics (mental), science became purely objective. In medicine, the body was approached from a very mechanical approach and the doctor/patient relationship was diminished. Belief and faith were discounted on their influence on healing.

Can you see the direct opposing thoughts of these philosophies of Locke and Descartes? The blank slate theorists believed that the external world was the most important part of life that shaped us, and the ghost in the machine theorists believed that it was all internal. Here is how I see it: Locke's philosophies coincide with the expressive's values (outer-feeler), and Descartes's philosophies are like the analytical's (inner-thinker). It is duality in its finest. Let's explore the next two camps of human nature philosophies that have helped create the world we live in.

Pinker goes on and describes a third theory of human nature, which is called the noble savage. This theory believes that people are naturally selfless, peaceable, and untroubled. We become corrupted only by exposure to society. Thus, we are not responsible for what we are because society made us who we are. The theory espouses the idea that if society can control behavior deliberately, then it can dominate all social problems. We see this theory in action with our present-day political correctness, which is so pervasive.

This theory has as its originator Jean-Jacques Rousseau (1712–1778) who was a philosopher of the Enlightenment. His political ideas influenced the French Revolution, along with the concepts of democracy and socialism. He believed that a modern, industrialized society corrupted humankind by competition and greed and that the more men deviated from the state of nature, the worse off they would be. Rousseau thought that men would be free, wise, and good in the state of nature because of our instincts and emotions—when not distorted by the unnatural limitations of civilization.

The basis for modern democracy came from *The Social Contract* and *Discourse on Inequality*. Rousseau's writings stemmed from his perception of human nature. He believed that humans possessed a natural goodness and that caring for oneself did not exclude the concern from the welfare of others.

He also believed that all people were socially equal, which played an important role in the present-day promotion of human rights. He endorsed direct democracy in which every citizen had an equal responsibility to agree on the laws that governed them, and he argued against the idea that monarchs were divinely empowered to rule.

The polar opposite philosophical theory was discussed by Pinker in his book, but he seemed to discount it as a viable category of thought. Thomas Hobbes (1588–1679) believed just the opposite of Rousseau and wrote about his particular theories of human nature. Hobbes saw people as naturally wretched and acting entirely from their own self-interests without regard for others. He said that fear was the greatest determining fact in human life.

He did not believe there was a soul or mind that was separate from the body and humans basically pursued their own self-interests by avoiding pain and seeking pleasure. Hobbes felt that in the natural world only the strong would survive unless order was imposed by a greater power. He believed that a sovereign ruler with absolute power was necessary for creating a peaceful society and thus was the best form of government.

In his classic 1651 book *Leviathan,* Hobbes advocated that all members of society submit to one absolute central authority for the sake of peace, and by doing so, they would prevent a civil war and ultimately their demise. In *Leviathan,* he established a social contract theory that has since become the foundation for most Western political philosophy. You can see this in action today by our government creating and enforcing laws to control the masses. Our government, our legal system, our military, and law enforcement entities all have their philosophies based upon Hobbes work.

Pinker did not label this last human nature theory, but we must call it something in order to bring it alive and illustrate its influence in our world. It is the polar opposite to the noble savage, which believed in our natural innate goodness as a species. This theory believes that the masses must be controlled for their own good or else there would be chaos and destruction if left to their own devices. A single sovereign ruler would control its subjects out of a need for societies' survival.

After much deliberation, I have labeled this theory of human nature the masses of minions. The masses of minions theory believes in the inability of humans to control themselves and thus they must be controlled by a higher authority with ultimate power.

I see that the noble savage theory has the values of the amiables as it is all about the people and the masses of minions is all about an efficient controlling authority, which has the values of the drivers. Here we have the sources of another conflict of duality in our world.

A Unified Theory of Human Nature

We now have four competing and conflicting theories of human nature that correspond to the four competing and conflicting forces of nature we have been discussing:

1. Noble savage (an amiable perspective)
2. Blank slate (an expressive point of view)
3. Masses of minions (drivers in control)
4. Ghost in the machine (analytical thinking)

I believe all of these theories are true and valid from their individual points of reference. But each of them is incomplete in terms of the big picture. What if we applied what we have learned about the necessity of unity to create a whole new theory of human nature? A unified theory that entails all of these opposing and competing theories would give us a model that is complete and universal. Wouldn't that explain it all? Just as importantly, it would fit into our model of competing values.

Human nature is complex because of these conflicting and competing values, right? If we see the world from one of these theories' points of view, then we are obviously missing out on what the other theories help us understand. Just like the four seasons, each has their own value in the grand scheme of life; these four theories of human nature also have their place in our understanding of who we are. Here is a brief rundown and my thoughts of the theories:

- The noble savage says we are innately good at birth, but society negatively influences us. I can go along with that for the majority of people. I can agree that society sometimes doesn't do us any good and can have the power that may corrupt our goodness.

- The blank slate states that we are created by our environment—and we are influenced by nurture, not by our nature. I can definitely see how we are shaped by our parents, peers, schooling, and culture. The external environment is a huge influence on how we live.

- The masses of minions believes we aren't capable of controlling our lives, and left alone, we would all be fighting amongst ourselves, leading to ultimate destruction. I have to admit that we need rules and regulations that can only come from government—as long as the government is by and for the people and does not become oppressive.

- The ghost in the machine theory believes that our minds and souls are distinct from our bodies, and they give us free will, choice, and the personal responsibility to create our selves and our lives. From my analytical viewpoint, this makes a lot of sense.

Conclusion: we now have some real understanding of the competing forces of nature that shape our world, including our Mother Nature's seasons, the temperaments, commerce, individual balance, leadership, and the philosophical basis for our perceptions. Our model of competing values seems to be omnipresent in our world. Unity of these competing values appears to be the answer we have been searching for.

Our next summary poem attempts to bring it all together.

Unity of opposites is the piece that's been omitted
If you really want solutions, you must be committed
To swallowing your pride and listening to your opponent
'Cause you're just a small bit of the larger component.

What the world needs now are people who are united.
Playing games that divide is just plain shortsighted.
We are stuck in a rut while debating who is right,
Choosing our sides and ending up in a fight.

Arguing and fussing is always so depleting,
Conflicting values in nature are competing.
Let's take a hint from our own Nature's Mother,
Opposing temperaments truly complement one another.

The entirety of this world has been created a wonder,
While most of humanity has been led asunder.
Divided we'll fall while united we'll thrive,
It's the solution we need for all to survive.

Lesson 5

Shopping for Values

Values are like fingerprints. Nobody's the same, but
you leave 'em all over everything you do.
—Elvis Presley

We have been talking about competing values and how they shape our world. Let's explore values and develop a real understanding of what they are. Values are an internally held set of enduring beliefs, preferences, motivators, and ideals that basically drive us and guide us as individuals. They bring meaning and purpose to our lives. Values go hand in hand with our emotions. Our values are an expression of our emotions and our feelings. In fact, if there is not an emotional attachment to a particular value, then it is really not a value for that particular person.

Plato recognized the importance of values in our lives and went so far as to come up with a list of values he believed people should adopt and live by. This was done 2,400 years ago. He understood the meaning and value of "good" values so very long ago.

Values are an important aspect of understanding human nature since they are possibly the key drivers of our actions. In other words, people do what they do because of the values they hold dear. In order to understand human nature, we have to get a handle on what values are and what they mean. Remember that our values always have emotional attachments.

The most important lesson to learn is that values are subjective. By definition, values cannot be proven superior to one or another. Also, they can't be proven true by scientific methods. If something can be proven scientifically, it isn't a value. But they impact every aspect of our lives and our choices, decisions, and directions. So what are values—and where do we get them?

Everybody has his or her own set of values. If values are subjective and are not able to be proven better or worse than another, then who is right and who is wrong when it comes to a difference in values? All of us are justified in thinking and feeling the ways we do because of the values that run us. If we are judging ourselves, we are always justified in doing what we do. Everybody feels that way, but sometimes we are the only ones who understand ourselves because we are the only ones who have the value systems we do. It also makes it very easy to judge others when we can't understand their justifications for their actions.

Value systems are very complicated to explain. They are a complex and integrated web of interpreted experiences and genetically programmed preferences. Are values a result of nature or nurture? Scientists, philosophers, and researchers have tried to explore this mystery for centuries. Both sides have valid arguments, but we are beginning to get some answers to this question.

The question of free will versus a predetermined fate is an offspring from this debate and really underscores our interpretations of the meaning of life. This is pretty heavy stuff to ponder. For now, let's just figure out what values are and what they mean to our daily lives.

So Many Different Values!

Just look at this list of values; see how many there are and how many combinations of values people can hold. Hold on to your hat; there's a bunch of them! And you can add many more values to this list. I think you get the point after glancing over them. Here goes ...

abundance acceptance accessibility accomplishment accuracy achievement acknowledgment activeness adaptability adoration adroitness adventure affection affluence aggressiveness agility alertness altruism ambition amusement anticipation appreciation approachability articulacy assertiveness assurance attentiveness attractiveness audacity availability awareness awe balance beauty being the best belonging benevolence bliss boldness bravery brilliance buoyancy calmness camaraderie candor capability care carefulness celebrity certainty challenge charity charm chastity cheerfulness clarity cleanliness clear-mindedness cleverness closeness comfort commitment compassion completion composure concentration confidence conformity congruency connection consciousness consistency contentment continuity contribution control conviction conviviality coolness cooperation cordiality correctness courage courtesy craftiness creativity credibility cunning curiosity daring decisiveness decorum deference delight dependability depth desire determination devotion devoutness dignity diligence direction directness discipline discovery discretion diversity dominance dreaming drive duty dynamism eagerness economy ecstasy education effectiveness efficiency elation elegance empathy encouragement endurance energy enjoyment entertainment enthusiasm excellence excitement exhilaration expectancy expediency experience expertise exploration expressiveness extravagance extroversion exuberance fairness faith fame family fascination fashion fearlessness ferocity fidelity fierceness financial independence firmness fitness flexibility flow fluency focus fortitude frankness freedom friendliness frugality fun gallantry generosity gentility giving grace gratitude gregariousness growth guidance happiness harmony health heart helpfulness heroism holiness honesty honor hopefulness hospitality humility humor hygiene imagination impact impartiality independence industry ingenuity inquisitiveness insightfulness inspiration integrity intelligence intensity intimacy intrepidness introversion intuition intuitiveness inventiveness investing joy judiciousness justice keenness knowledge leadership learning liberation liberty lightheartedness liveliness logic love loyalty majesty making a difference mastery maturity meekness mellowness meticulousness mindfulness modesty motivation mysteriousness neatness nerve obedience open-mindedness openness optimism order organization originality outlandishness outrageousness passion peace perceptiveness perfection perkiness perseverance persistence persuasiveness philanthropy piety playfulness pleasantness pleasure poise polish popularity potency power practicality pragmatism precision preparedness presence privacy proactivity professionalism prosperity prudence punctuality purity realism reason reasonableness recognition recreation refinement reflection relaxation reliability religiousness resilience resolution resolve resourcefulness respect responsibility rest restraint reverence richness rigor sacredness sacrifice sagacity saintliness satisfaction security self-control selflessness self-reliance sensitivity sensuality serenity service sexuality sharing shrewdness significance silence silliness simplicity sincerity skillfulness solidarity solitude soundness speed spirit spirituality spontaneity spunk stability stealth stillness strength structure success support supremacy surprise sympathy synergy teamwork temperance thankfulness thoroughness thoughtfulness thrift tidiness timeliness traditionalism tranquility transcendence trust trustworthiness truth understanding unflappability uniqueness unity usefulness utility valor variety victory virtue vision vitality vivacity warmth watchfulness wealth willfulness willingness winning wisdom wittiness wonder youthfulness zeal (Thanks to Steve Pavlina at Stevepavlina.com for compiling this list.)

Everyone has a large set of these values that creates the person they are. Plus, everyone has a different set of these values. Wow! Can you see why people are so complex and difficult to understand? It is truly an answer to one of the major secrets of human nature.

The fact of the matter is that our values run us like a program runs a computer. But we all have a different program. No one is alike. No one has completely the same values. Human beings are like snowflakes; no two are the same.

How We Choose

One of the guiding principles of psychology is that people are generally motivated to behave in ways that lead to positive feelings, and they tend to avoid behaviors that lead to discomfort or pain. Values are one of the main underlying determinates of these feelings. We feel good if we comply with our values and feel bad if we don't.

Motivational theorists believe that there is an underlying "cause" for every act or behavior. These causes can be reduced to a neurological component where chemical and electrical actions in the brain start, modify, and maintain specific human behaviors with positive reward reinforcement.

One of the main motivational causes is the release of a chemical called dopamine that makes us feel good. Things that stimulate the release of dopamine include food, comfort, possessions, entertainment, affection, sex, and social dominance. Dopamine is also a major component for addictive behaviors, drives, emotions, and impulsive actions.

On the other end of the spectrum, fear can be the main reason in our decision-making process that makes us choose against something. Our brains are designed with built-in protection mechanisms that provide a flight-or-fight response to things that might hurt or endanger us.

Fear can be hardwired into our brains; some of it is instinctual, and some of it is learned. It can be a lifesaver for us, or it can block us from doing what we know we should do. It is imperative that we understand where our fears come from. Fear is one of our six basic emotions, and everyone has this built-in emotion for survival.

The brain consists of three different brains actually. One of our brains is responsible for our bodies functioning properly and its survival. This brain is also called the reptilian brain because it is no different than those types of animal's brains. It controls the body functions required for sustaining life, such as breathing and body temperature.

It also is responsible for the flight-or-fight response, which is imperative for animals to survive. Unfortunately, the least evolved portion of our brains can also exert the most control over our actions. Fear impulses are centered in our reptilian brains, and there are many reasons why they are activated. Survival and self-protection are just a few examples.

Fear of going to the dentist can elicit the same feelings as if we thought we were going to be attacked by a predator—even if the fear is unjustified with the rational part of our brains. We all have fears that can immobilize us to choose irrationally. It has been said that when we overcome a fear of ours, the brain evolves and makes completely new connections.

But I have some patients who never get over their fears. To me, it means that their brains have well developed neural pathways that keep these impulses strong and active. Overcoming fear is a very uncomfortable task for human beings. It also could possibly be one of our most important.

Our brains are hardwired for seeking pleasure and avoiding pain, but everyone's ideas about pain and pleasure are different. This is a major contributor to our behavior and our choices. Could our values also be a result of the way our brains are hardwired or are our brains hardwired as a result of our values? It's kind of a what-came-first thing: the chicken or the egg.

Dr. William Glasser has been a renowned psychiatrist, author, lecturer, and is the developer of choice therapy. In his book *Choice Theory*, he states that all human behaviors are an attempt to satisfy five basic needs: survival, power, belonging, freedom, and enjoyment. This is different from classic stimulus-response theories that don't account for these underlying motivators. Glasser's five basic needs can also be called values. He claims that these are genetically programmed by birth.

He says that we have no choice but to feel bad when one of our needs isn't met, and we feel good when a need is satisfied. When any need is unsatisfied, we will behave in ways to get it fulfilled.

There are two points I have gotten from Dr. Glasser's work. The first one is that our genetics determine so much of our wants and needs. The second is that if you look closely at the five basic needs, you will see that four of them mimic the values of our four basic temperaments:

- belonging—amiable
- enjoyment—expressive
- power—driver
- freedom—analytical

In my opinion, this is another confirmation for the importance of the T-Code. The other basic need he described is survival, which is much more than a value; it's a basic instinctual function of anything that lives.

Cultural and Family Values

Our external environment has a huge influence on the creation of our value systems. As we are growing up, we depend almost entirely upon external validation from our families and society to determine what is right and wrong. This is one of the areas in life where the blank slate theory of human nature is validated.

Our morals and ethics are a reflection of what others tell us. This helps explain how cultures are formed differently from various locations, regions, and nations. Culture is defined as the sum total of learned behaviors of a group of people that results from a cumulative deposit of values that are created by knowledge, experiences, beliefs, attitudes, concepts, religion, language, etc.

Culture is handed down from generation to generation. We are at the mercy of our culture to a certain degree for how we view the world. Cultural pressure to conform is enormous and affects us in ways that are too numerable to mention. Some examples are the ways we dress, speak, eat, drink, work, and play; these are mostly determined by our culture. It would be hard to ignore the effect it has on us.

Our family environment has more influence on our values of religious beliefs, political orientations (whether conservative or liberal), work ethics, and interpersonal relationships. How we view, act, and interpret our relationships have their foundation here. Our relationship with our parents sets the stage for all other relationships in our lives.

When you look at the many variables with cultural and family influences, then throw in our genetic predeterminations and personal experiences, you can see how complicated all human beings are. You never know what has shaped the values in each of us. Thinking about this subject makes my head spin!

My wife and I have almost completely different sets of values. Some of them were probably shaped by our families and the cultures that were present during our development. But I think that a lot of them just come naturally with our different temperaments. If you study the characteristics of the T-Code, you can also translate them into values. I believe that these types of values are preprogrammed and hardwired into us by our genetics. It would be next to impossible to overcome these values.

I value achievement, accomplishment, ambition, creativity, determination, financial independence, freedom, industry, peace, preparedness, relaxation, responsibility, self-control, success, tranquility, understanding, and wisdom.

My wife values affection, appreciation, assertiveness, attractiveness, control, elegance, entertainment, family, friendliness, fun, lightheartedness, love, openness, recreation, recognition, spontaneity, and youthfulness.

And these are both short lists just to give you an idea about how different we are. With these differences, where is our common ground? Why can our marriage work when so many others with lesser differences don't? I think that ours works because we both love each other, and we truly value the relationship and place it above everything else. Who knows why it works. Maybe it's just that I know it's cheaper to keep her!

> "Marriage is not a simple love affair, it's an ordeal, and the ordeal is the
> sacrifice of the ego to a relationship in which two have become one."
> —Joseph Campbell, *The Power of the Myth*

Some of our values change throughout our lives, and we obviously do also. A lot of our values are formed from the experiences we go through and the lessons we learn. As we grow up, so do the maturity of our values.

They say it's normal for us to go through a values change every seven years or so. That means that in a marriage, you may not end up with the same person you married. That's hard for a lot of marriages. How many times do you hear couples say, "We just grew apart," when they get divorced? Sounds like they couldn't handle the values change. In the seven-year itch—where people start to stray in their marriages—values probably change too.

We have shared values that keep people together in ways other than marriages. Group values bring people together in a number of ways. Think about teenagers and the peer pressure to conform. They have a set of pretty strict values they have to abide by. If they don't conform, they risk alienation. For a teen, this is a fate worse than death.

The group's values—whether they are good things or not—set the standards of behavior. How many parents have wrestled with this situation but are almost powerless to overcome the control of the group's influence?

As parents, we strive to instill values that are important to us into our children so they will benefit from our experiences. And our values are the right ones, right? Of course!

Think back to when you were growing up, and try to remember what it was like. I have to believe that all of us grew up with peer pressure of some kind. It is easy to recognize when you look back. It isn't so easy to recognize when you are under its spell.

But thankfully, we grew up, and a lot of our values changed as we matured. I remember that looking, acting, and talking like the group of guys I hung around with was about as important as anything I could think of. I believe that it's probably true for most kids growing up.

As we grow and mature, some of our values change. Our perspectives on life change too. Values, being subjective, are subject to change. But my observation is that our values associated with our temperaments won't change much if any throughout our life.

Values and Duality

I want you to start thinking about the duality in values. We have discussed how temperaments are based upon certain dualities. I say that all values are also based upon dualities.

Try to recognize what values are most important to you and then find the ones that are least important to you. I bet you will find that your most important values and your least important values are opposite in some way.

It is in our nature as humans to form groups, clubs, organizations, and societies with others who share similar values. We are validated and vindicated when we gather with people who think or feel the same as we do about important issues. There is nothing wrong with this except that in our present way of being, our groups are usually formed in opposition to other groups who don't feel or think the way we do.

These conflicts of values set up divisions that affect our society in many ways. Being with more people who think or feel like we do will help us believe we are right. In a Salon.com interview, legal scholar Cass Sunstein said, "I think it's a very firm part of human nature that if you surround yourself with like-minded people, you'll end up thinking more extreme versions of what you thought before." What a great observation!

These divisions of conflict are nothing more than duality in action. I'm here to tell you that this duality thing is everywhere in the world. I can't emphasize how important it is to us experiencing life. Once again, everything in the world has its opposite in order to give it meaning. It also allows for conflict in every aspect of our lives with almost anyone. Somewhere, there will always be someone who disagrees with your choices.

Before you are in a relationship you usually never have a chance to see how your ways can be so conflicting with another's ways. But never lose sight of the fact that your values are important to you and hold them dear.

At the same time, remember that someone else's values are just as important to them. Our lesson is to try to not always fight about who is right and who is wrong. How important is it to uncover our values? It may be the key to more than just self-discovery.

> Achievement of your happiness is the only moral purpose of your life, and that happiness, not pain or mindless self-indulgence, is proof of your moral integrity, since it is the proof and the result of your loyalty to the achievement of your values.
> —Ayn Rand, *The Virtue of Selfishness*

I believe that this quote reveals so much about our humanness. It holds the key to so much of our well-being. We sometimes spend so much energy and time in mindless self-indulgence or doing what others tell us what we should be doing instead of trying to achieve our values. Because of these things we may lose sight of what is really important.

Our summary poem takes on this very difficult subject of values. I hope it helps to get a grasp of just how important values are to our being human.

A value system runs you and all of your actions
Your hopes, your dreams, what gives you satisfaction.
This system is in you, in your mind, in your head.
It tells you what's good and all that you dread.

Just like your computer, there's loaded software.
That plays in your brain; it's the way you're aware.
We're all uniquely programmed; that's easy to see.
But accepting each other is not our cup of tea.

"How can they do this?" we ask with subjection.
"Why don't they do that?" we voice the correction.
But aren't we justified in doing what we do every day?
"Just don't you judge me," we are likely to say.

Everyone is so different; it's all too confusing.
The conflict we have here, we're always defusing.
Our lives are journeys that continue to unfold.
We go down our own paths because of the values we hold.

Lesson 6

Quality and Temperaments

All of life is a dispute over taste and tasting.
—Friedrich Nietzsche, *Thus Spake Zarathustra*

Don't you just know when you really like something? Where does this thought or feeling come from? And why does it differ so much from one person to another? You see it everywhere. A friend tells you about a great new movie he just saw. You go see it, and you think it stinks. Or it could be a restaurant, a car, music, anything. There truly is no accounting for taste.

So quality is something that is not a constant or a universal evaluation of anything. In fact, the very term quality is one of the most overworked words in advertising and marketing. We all say when we like something that it's *good*. But whatever *it* is, it really isn't where quality begins. It's within each of us. Our perception of quality is involved in every choice we make. We choose what we believe is best for us.

Why is a discussion of quality included in this book about human nature? At first, it may seem somewhat unrelated, but in truth, it is at the center of just about everything we do. If you think about it, our lives are all about searching for what we like and disregarding things we dislike. This statement is more profound than you can even imagine. I will try to elaborate on this as the book unfolds. Why do we like what we like? And why do we dislike what we do? We will probably never fully know the answers to these questions but it shouldn't stop us from seeking more understanding of this profound subject. Let's begin our inquiry of quality with its dissection which just happens to have the duality theme that is so pervasive in human nature.

In Robert Pirsig's classic *Zen and the Art of Motorcycle Maintenance*, the search for the meaning of quality ended in the conclusion that it was neither just a subjective feeling nor just an objective thought. It was the culmination of them both. The way people perceive quality is how they feel subjectively and how they think objectively. It's a fusion of the two when both of your brains, left and right, can agree on something.

You just know that something is of quality, sometimes without any conscious decision making process. In his book Pirsig labels this as *a priori* knowledge. It is a knowing without having actual experience of the situation. A great example of this is love at first sight.

How do you do something as important and life changing as falling in love the very first time you meet that special someone? It doesn't make any logical sense. I can testify that it is possible because that is what happened when I first met my wife. My father also had this happen to him with my mom.

Another example, albeit a less dramatic one, is going to a store and finding something that you have to buy on the spot. You didn't set out to make a purchase of that sort but when you saw it, you just had to buy it. Where do these decisions come from? Our personal perception of quality has to come into the picture for these examples. We just know when something is right for us. Then again, sometimes we don't. Let me explain.

Our experience of quality is very complex and sometimes irrational. There was an important study done by Hilke Plassmann from the California Institute of Technology that helps us see another aspect of our perceptions of quality. Her work shows how our perceptions can be altered by external sources, sometimes without us being aware. Sometimes our decisions of quality may not be rational or intelligent.

A wine-tasting experiment was done to see if the price of a wine had anything to do with the perception of its quality. In other words, are we influenced into believing something is better than another just because it has a higher price tag?

For the experiment, the participants were told that they would taste a number of wines to test their differences in their taste perception. But what they really did was taste the same exact wines, just out of different bottles. They were told that one was priced ten dollars and the other bottle was priced at ninety dollars, but the only difference in the wine was the perceived price.

Instead of just asking the participants their verbal opinions of the wine, MRI scans were done of their brains while tasting. They found that the area of the brain that is mostly related to pleasure sensations was lit up on the scans when the "higher-priced wine" was tasted. Can you see how savvy marketers can manipulate us by just making their products more expensive? Can you see that our decision-making processes might not be all that astute or accurate?

Another example of how our perception of quality can be altered is by the advertising we are subjected to. There is one reason that advertisers use celebrities to help them sell their products; they help raise our perceptions of quality for their products or services. The quality of the product really has nothing to do with perception in this case. We are just influenced by the celebrity who supposedly uses the product.

Quality can be altered in a number of ways as we receive new information that involves our ability to judge things. So quality is never a constant because subjectivity and objectivity are always subject to change. That being said, there are components of quality that are consistent and help us to more fully understand what quality is all about.

The Components of Service Quality

Quality shows up for us in all sorts of ways. As a dentist who aspired to succeed, I wanted to deliver quality in my practice. I knew from some of my miserable experiences with my early team relationships that quality was not just how well my technical dentistry turned out; it was the entire service experience and the patients' perception of how well they were taken care of.

Being so interested in improving my understanding of this subject, I teamed up with a good buddy of mine I'd known since grade school. He was a professor at the University of Missouri where I did my undergraduate studies (majoring in drinking beer). Dr. Gregg Martin and I decided to do a research study of patients' perceptions of quality service in dentistry. We did a survey with more than six thousand patients participating across the nation and came up with some interesting results—some of which helped me in developing the T-Code.

Gleaning information from a well-known business book, *Delivering Quality Service*, we concluded that there are four aspects of service quality. Two of them are subjective or feeling components of quality. These are empathy and responsiveness. The other two are objective or thinking components concerning quality. They are capability and reliability.

We noticed that the dimensions of service quality correspond to the dualities of the four basic temperaments of the T-Code. This was another verification of how universal our competing values model is in our world. This is the main point I want to try to illustrate here.

Let's get to know these dimensions a little better, and we'll see how quality service is created by a combination of all the four temperament's attributes:

- empathy (understanding and identifying with another person's situation, motives and feelings)—attribute of an amiable
- responsiveness (quick to respond or react to wants and needs) is an outer feeling—like an expressive
- reliability (the state of doing things right) is concerned with outer thinking—a driver thing
- capability (having the knowledge and skill to do the task) is an inner thinking function—definitely analytical

Now we can see how all the temperament's positive attributes are necessary for quality service to be achieved.

Since everyone feels differently and thinks differently based upon his or her temperament and life experiences, it follows that quality can be perceived as different for each of us. And since feelings can change and thinking can be modified by acquiring new information, quality is always changing. That's why it's probably unwise for a business to keep doing the same thing over and over for years and expect the same results, especially in today's world where everything changes so fast!

Of course, we don't normally go through all this processing consciously when we perceive something as quality. We just know it when we see it. And if any of these dimensions of quality has been overlooked or is insufficient, then people will sense it unconsciously and react accordingly. Any business in the service arena must be aware of these dimensions, especially in the business environment of today.

When selecting a professional to help you in any area of real importance, don't you want the very best? Aren't you looking for someone you can really trust … who represents quality … who is competent (objective) and caring (subjective)?

For an extreme example, let's imagine you find it necessary to have major surgery and you're getting ready to go into the operating room. What would be going on in your head if your surgeon were very caring but fresh out of med school?

Or your doctor was very experienced but seemed somewhat uncaring—maybe even joking with the nurses about the recent party and not devoting his attention to you as you're nervously awaiting surgery? You get the idea.

Our research results were not only enlightening but very instructive on what it takes to be a quality service provider. It showed us just how important it is to the consumer that all of these dimensions of quality have to be done to their satisfaction. By fulfilling their expectations the consumer is able to develop a level of trust that keeps them coming back for more. Developing trust is mandatory for a doctor–patient relationship. It is the ultimate expression of quality in this situation. Let's look at trust and how to achieve it.

Trust is the result of both competence and caring. It is the marriage of both right and left brains: the union of the subjective and the objective. This is just as Pirsig concluded.

To be competent, you have to be both capable and reliable. These are both objective, left-brain thinking components, and they are expressed in a tangible manner. These are two of the service quality dimensions that our research demonstrated.

To be caring, you have to be both empathetic and responsive to each person's individual needs. These are the other two dimensions that are subjective, right-brain feeling components and are expressed emotionally.

This all demonstrated to me that in order to be a really good dentist, I was going to have to be a reliable, capable professional that was also empathetic and responsive to my patient's needs. That is a tall order to fill for anyone! If I was going to earn my patient's trust, I was going to have to work hard in the dimensions that didn't come naturally to me.

Once again, it all goes back to the secrets of the T-Code. Each of the temperaments is better suited to handle one of these dimensions of quality. And once again, it demonstrates the value of each basic temperament—each kind of person who makes up humankind. But we still need to remember that we, as individuals, are just pieces of the big picture puzzle and that the best results in life are when the opposites are in harmony.

Surprise, Surprise!

When Dr. Gregg Martin and I finished our research on what people think about quality service in dentistry, I had an idea I thought could be developed into a profitable side business. Because we had accumulated so much data from dentists and their patients, we had a way to test, compare, and rank dentists on this important subject.

We could tell dentists their strengths to build upon and their weaknesses from their patients' perspectives so they could target exactly where and how to improve their practices. The business failed but not through a lack of effort on our part. It turned out dentists simply didn't recognize (or understand the importance) that they needed help in these areas, especially when our research proved that the dimensions of empathy and responsiveness ranked highest in the patients' perception of quality.

In short, we were trying to sell something no one wanted. Not a good business plan. These highest-ranking dimensions by patients were those of subjective feelings. Most dentists are analyticals who are drawn to technical and scientific things.

Stepping into uncomfortable areas, such as feelings and subjectivity, wasn't high on their long to-do lists. Most dentists see their profession through technical lenses. Looking at things subjectively may be uncomfortable and unnatural. Buying a service that isn't valued isn't going to happen for dentists—or anyone else.

The business master Peter Drucker studied this subject long and hard. From his classic book, *Innovation and Entrepreneurship*, he gives us further insight:

> "Quality in a product or service is not what the supplier puts in. It is what the customer gets out and is willing to pay for. A product is not quality because it is hard to make and costs a lot of money, as manufacturers typically believe. This is incompetence. Customers pay only what is of use to them and gives them value. Nothing else constitutes quality."

I wish I had heard these words before we started our little side business. I could have saved a lot of time and energy. Lesson learned.

Dentists aren't different from most of us in seeking knowledge within our own comfort zones and avoiding those that conflict with our natures. Have you ever heard of starving artists? They're probably starving because they're so into art they neglect the most basic elements of what it takes to make a living. How many military officers are warm and fuzzy? Are librarians usually outgoing socialites? You get the point.

The people in any walk of life who have learned through desire or necessity to step out of their comfort zones are probably the most successful individuals. These are the people who strive for excellence in many areas and have learned these T-Code lessons on their own.

Masterminding Quality

Napoleon Hill was the author of *Think and Grow Rich*, one of the most influential self-help books of all time. He also wrote *Law of Success,* which came from him interviewing and learning from the most important and successful businesspeople of his day. He learned from these elite men that a mastermind group was one of the tools they used to solve problems and create new innovations to help them in their endeavors.

The mastermind group was made up of successful people from different careers with differing backgrounds and perspectives. Working together, the group was able to create new possibilities and solve problems by using this quality approach. Their empires were built using this as one of their secrets of success.

The mastermind principle was built on the old adage that two heads are better than one. The mastermind group utilized the many different perspectives of its members to arrive at solutions that would not have been formulated by individuals working alone. These mastermind meetings were an additional step in their process but they were well worth the extra effort it took to coordinate them. The creative potential of groups like this are enormous, according to Napoleon Hill.

One thing I have learned through my years of doing dentistry is that quality never happens by accident. It is always the result of planning, effort, intelligent direction, and skillful execution by me and every member of my team. Sometimes we just can't do things all by our self, nor should we.

A famous Zen koan (philosophical riddle) asks, "What is the sound of one hand clapping?" This Zen riddle has intrigued people for ages. My answer to it is there is no sound and that one hand can't accomplish a clap without another hand. That is an obvious answer, but I believe the riddle was made up to make us understand that one side is incomplete by itself. In life, nature needs its counterpart to successfully complete its purpose. Here we go; this duality thing comes up once again.

How important is this concept? How about the creation of life itself? The miracle of procreation is based totally on this concept. We are blessed with a child *only* with the union of a man and a woman. If this isn't a good enough example of what happens with opposites and their creative potential, then I don't know what is. Life is so mysterious, but we have significant clues about what we need to master our experience here. These clues are right under our noses.

What if we could apply this concept to solving our significant problems that we face in our world? What would happen if we truly understood that fighting to overcome our adversaries really hurts ourselves and inhibits the creative process that would benefit all involved? Instead of spending our efforts on overwhelming our opposites, we could come together to actually create something superior to what we want as individuals.

Up next is a flow chart that illustrates the duality nature of quality. You can see the opposing components that make up our perception of quality. The true lesson of this chart is to see that taking a side in a conflicting matter might negate the possibilities of the best outcome. It appears that we need opposing sides in order to truly achieve quality. Food for thought, for sure!

Dr Martin Luther King brought this to light in his book Strength to Love. He said, "Life at its best is a creative synthesis of opposites in fruitful harmony." Amen! This is my favorite quote of all time. So much is revealed in just a few words. In fact, this short quote holds the key to conflict and the solution to the problems facing humanity. Thank you, Dr. King!

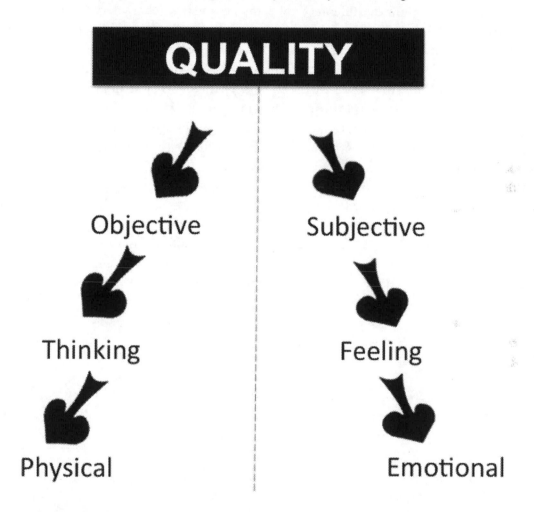

This chart shows that quality is made up of all the opposites we have been discussing so far. We can even go as far as relating our right brains and left brains to this chart. We need both sides represented when quality is to be found, created, or achieved. We can't have real quality without the opposites and the conflicting dualities as part of the process.

You might be thinking that history is full of examples of geniuses who individually created works of art, music, literature, innovations, scientific accomplishments, etc. It has been postulated that the great thinkers and doers of the world have better connections between the two hemispheres of their brains than normal people do. We could call them whole brained rather than just right- or left-brain oriented. They use the joining of their own internal opposites for their creative processes.

We might be able to tap into this potential if we learn some of the lessons that the T-Code has given us by understanding the components of quality.

Now you have seen how the different temperaments and their characteristics shape so much of our lives in such important ways, such as our interpersonal relationships, our places in the scheme of things, our effectiveness in business, the creative process, and our perceptions of quality. I hope this proves helpful for understanding and appreciating the fact that everyone plays a vital role in this world and that we need each other. Keep this concept in mind as you read further.

I believe that quality is one of the main drivers in our evolutionary progression as human beings. Quality leads us in a direction that will ultimately change and shape the world. It isn't something that we really have control over. We are evolving with quality as our guide. Quality will lead us to become more than we presently are.

This concept gives us a great understanding of how we evolve and our personal connections to evolution when we choose excellence. When we personally choose excellence in whatever we do in life, we are choosing to be a part of humanity's evolutionary process. Quality is the evolutionary roadmap that will guide us through the maze of life into the uncharted future.

I was a bit apprehensive to write a summary poem for this chapter because of the complexity of the subject. I think it turned out okay. But you decide, because your perception of quality is your own.

Seeking quality in life will hold us accountable,
With the problems we face that seem insurmountable.

Helping humanity in a way that is enjoyed,
Keeps us in demand and gainfully employed.

Doing things right, staying ahead of the rest,
Makes us more competent, and becoming our best.

We learn to treat people with compassion and empathy,
To give of ourselves when they might need some sympathy.

Quality is the mother of all of these things,
Pursuing excellence is the ultimate life brings.

Service to others, the highest goal we achieve,
When it's all said and done, it's our legacy to leave.

Lesson 7

Simplifying the Complicated

Knowledge is a process of piling up facts; wisdom lies in their simplification.
—Martin H. Fisher, *Encore: A Continuing Anthology*

Life is strange because people are strange. But the more you learn about what makes people do the things they do, the less strange and less complicated they become. In order to further understand human nature, we need to recognize two more dualities that shape our humanity.

Up to now, we have talked about the four basic types of people—amiables, expressives, analyticals, and drivers. We have compared them to the four seasons of nature. But as you know, not every day of a particular season is the same. There are a few constant variations that make our days different.

The basic four temperaments concept is useful, of course, but it's no surprise that people are more complicated than that. I think we have all figured out that people are very difficult to understand. This is verified by the fact that scientists and researchers now describe sixteen different personality types or temperaments. A number of books have been written on the subject.

Probably best known of these is *Please Understand Me* by David Keirsey and Marilyn Bates. It was my first exposure to this kind of information. When I read about the sixteen types in this book, it actually changed my life by changing how I viewed people. Understanding the information these researchers presented opened up a whole new world for me.

For the first time, I understood the differences in people and how they functioned. Most of all, it registered that they cannot help being who they are—any more than I can help being who I am—and that I should honor and appreciate the differences. I couldn't have taken this monumental step in my life without this book and the work of the authors. In fact, much of what we are discussing about temperaments comes from their research.

The four basic temperaments are subdivided by two new dualities. Understanding these last two dualities may appear to be a little tedious, but they are critically important for developing tolerance and compassion for those who are different than we are. And actually, it is pretty simple to learn.

Two New Dualities Further Define Who We Are.

Yes, all amiables, all expressives, all analyticals, and all drivers are not alike. But they are not alike in predictable and wonderful ways that bring order, balance, and symmetry to our human interactions. Thanks to researchers like Katharine Briggs and her daughter Isabel Briggs Myers, we can identify two more dualities that can help us more fully understand ourselves and others with far greater precision.

In Carl Jung's *Psychological Types,* he first described these different types, then Myers and Briggs expounded upon them and created a temperament assessment that has been used extensively since the 1960s. Hundreds of studies have proved their work to be valid and reliable. I have taken their work and renamed and reorganized the types in a way I think is easier to understand.

Learning the four dualities allows us to recognize all the different types without having the tedious task of memorizing a list of sixteen. Once again, learning this information is very important because without an understanding of the fundamental building blocks of our temperaments, we would not be able to develop an understanding of the roots of our conflicts.

My wife and I have experienced firsthand all the differences in temperament two people can possibly have. It smacks us in the face every time we turn around. As if it isn't enough that I'm an inner-thinker and she's an outer-feeler, we found out early in our relationship there are many other ways to be in conflict.

Our clocks were set—or not set—at different times. I function best when I have a routine or structured environment where I can be most effective and efficient. Time is important to me, and I want to make the most of it by having a schedule and a purpose. She prefers things to be open, unencumbered by not having to do anything until she feels like doing it. She thrives on the spontaneous while I feel totally out of control and drained living like that. She loves vacations where she can come and go as she pleases. After a few days of that, I'm ready to get back to work where I can accomplish something.

If she had to do anything on a time schedule in a preplanned way, she would be unhappy. As a dentist with a strict schedule each day and firm guidelines, being too flexible is not a good option. For my free-spirited wife, boundaries and restrictions are a death sentence. But in her defense, if there is something that must be done, it will get done, but in her way—without preplanning.

I like to work on one project at a time. She'll get going on something, switch gears, start another project, and bounce around as she sees fit. And she'll start on things at the weirdest times, maybe right before we go to bed. When we have household chores together, our differences in style drive me crazy.

My solution is a simple one. At work, I am the boss. At home, she is the boss. If this sounds like I have surrendered to her, so be it. Napoleon Bonaparte described his relationship to his wife Josephine by saying, "I generally had to give in." I think I'm in good company here.

Accepting that, I have learned to be more flexible with handling her flexibility. Because of all this, I have also learned to become more flexible when possible with my staff at our dental office, which has paid off. Staff members are much happier, and our productivity continues to improve. I've learned you don't always have to be so rigid with everything to get things done.

Are You a Controller or a Flexer?

Welcome to our new T-Code duality: control versus flexibility. Or, as I like to call our people types: controllers versus flexers. The general population is split evenly as with our other dualities.

Half of people like things set a certain way and adhere to rules, regulations, structure, and schedules to help them with handling their lives. The other half is just the opposite and wants their lives to have minimal restrictions that would limit their choices at any given moment. They prefer spontaneity, flexibility, and freedom.

This duality creates even more ways for us to have conflicts and makes people seem complicated and difficult. Understanding these final temperament dualities will certainly help you understand them and yourself.

Which are you? To help you decide, here are descriptions that may help.

CONTROLLERS	FLEXERS
Structured	Open
Settled	Options
Decided	Opportunities
Fixed	Alternatives
Finalized	Spontaneous
Completed	Emerging
Urgency	Excitement

There is one more step—one more duality—to finalize who you are. Again, true to form, my marriage serves as a good example.

Another constant source of differences between my wife and me is what we focus our thoughts or feelings on and how it comes out in our conversations. She really thinks I'm wacko at times because I'm always thinking about what may happen in the future. I like to be prepared for future events. It's always been that way for me. I knew I wanted to be a dentist in the third grade; I have always been looking ahead and getting excited about future possibilities.

My wife, on the other hand, is grounded in the present and can make each moment a special one if she gets a chance. This lady sees everything and notices immediately if anything is out of place. I call her the discrepancy-finder and she can find any of mine in a hurry. She is like the big Eye of Mordor in *The Lord of the Rings*, scouring the landscape to see what is going on. I, on the other hand, am usually unaware of anything except what is going on in my head. Not surprisingly, I miss much of what is happening around me. I'd make a horrible witness to a crime scene, but my wife would pour out what occurred in infinite detail.

Our Last Duality—Nowers Versus Planners

Our last duality contrasts these two kinds of people: those who are primarily concerned with the here and now and those who mostly concerned with the future. We like to call this last duality: the nowers versus the planners. Here are some descriptions of each.

NOWERS	PLANNERS
Experience	Hunches
Past and present	Future
Realistic	Speculative
Perspiration	Inspiration
Actual	Possible
Down to earth	Head in the clouds
Utility	Fantasy
Practicality	Ingenuity
Sensible	Imaginative

Only about 20 percent of the population is planners. It's probably a good thing because the world can handle only so many people with their heads in the clouds. But these types are responsible for being prepared for the future and seeing the big picture. They are highly responsible. The present is less important to these folks because they're stimulated by future possibilities.

It follows that 80 percent is nowers who live in the present and seldom concentrate on long-term planning. They think, *How can I even think about tomorrow when I have so much to do today?* With these last two, we have all the dualities that define specifically who we are. They are at work within all the different temperaments.

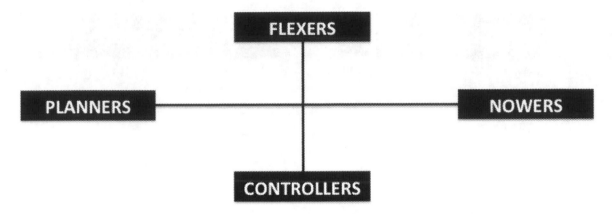

This gives us a framework on which to build the specific differences that define us all. Within each basic type—the amiables, expressives, analyticals, and drivers—we subdivide the types with these last two dualities and their four possibilities. They are:

(1) Planners-Flexors   (2) Nower-Flexers
(3) Planner-Controllers   (4) Nower-Controllers

You've seen each of these people. You're one of them yourself. Planner-flexers, for example, want to create the freedom to break down boundaries for a future of open possibilities. To simplify things even further, we label them adaptives.

The nower-flexers, on the other hand, want things loose and open in the present moment so they have the freedom to do and change as they see fit. We're calling them impulsives.

Planner-controllers seek to work out a strategy for specific future results. For us, they're Strategics.

The nower-controllers are largely concerned with today's events but have to be in control of what's going on. So they are by nature very comfortable in telling others what, when, where, and how to do something. They follow a strict set of rules and regulations that allow them to act quickly, without hesitation. We're calling them authoritatives. I had a group leader many years ago who would answer almost any question on any subject with the same statement. He always said, "Read and follow the rules!" He was a classic authoritative.

How the Modifiers Shape Final Temperament

These final two sets of dualities form four different "modifiers" that help shape who we are. We originated our temperament exploration with the original four types: amiables, expressives, drivers, and analyticals. These will continue to be our basic temperament types.

These four modifiers bring diversity and balance to each of the original types. They have the same distribution throughout the four basic types. They each have their own qualities and characteristics that help to add mystery to our understanding people. Once we understand how these modifiers work, we will be closer to mastering this subject.

Here are the four modifiers and how they contribute to our four basic temperaments.

FLEXERS

ADAPTIVES

Adaptives want to go with the flow in life. They search for identity, meaning, and significance. Tending to be idealistic, they seek to make the world a better place. They are enthusiastic about their ideas or causes that interest them. They put their many talents to work in the service of their ideals and morals.

IMPULSIVES

Impulsives treasure freedom to choose what's next. Needing to experience and act on their impulses, they strive to be graceful, bold, impressive and have an impact on their audience. Generally, they are excitable and optimistic — expecting lady luck to be on their side. So absorbed are they in the moment, they may lose sight of distant goals. They hunger for action and variety.

PLANNERS

NOWERS

STRATEGICS

Strategics seek knowledge, competence, achievement. They strive to understand what makes the world run and people tick. Thinking in terms of the future, they invent, design and define systems that will bring all a better future of their vision. Lost in their future thinking, they can miss present opportunities. They value individualism rather than emulating the group.

AUTHORITATIVES

Authoritatives desire responsibility and accountability. Expecting others to do the same, they have little patience for those who don't. Service and duty are very important to them. Their focus is on maintaining establishments and standard operating procedures. Looking to the past, they are serious minded and distrust chance.

CONTROLLERS

The final result is sixteen temperament groups that define us all—as well as where in life we fit and what kinds of professions best suit us. Humanity is made up of the sixteen different temperaments interacting to create the world as we know it.

The sheer beauty and absolute perfection of all this can be seen in the traits of each basic temperament and how the great subdivide further places them in their specialty areas. With the ability to divide each of the four temperaments in the same fashion, we have an easy way to remember the different sixteen types.

First recognize which of the four basic types they are, which is really easy, and then see if they are a flexer or controller. Finally check for their planner-nower duality. This one may be the most difficult to recognize. Planners are just a little different from the crowd since they think about a bigger picture than the nowers. Maybe they are a bit deeper, if that helps to describe them.

This next chart shows the equal divisions amongst each basic type. Because of the equal divisions, there is a balance of conflicts within the basic temperaments as well as the entire T-Code.

T-CODE TYPES

AMIABLES

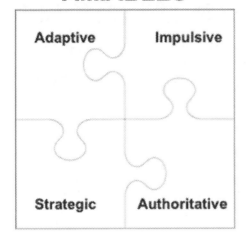

EXPRESSIVES

ANALYTICALS

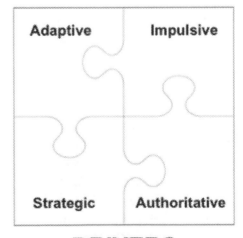

DRIVERS

It is a simply amazing system! There can be conflict between the internal divisions of each basic temperaments as well as similarities between the divisions of all the basic temperament types.

Because there are the same modifiers in each of the four basic temperaments, there are opportunities for the sub-types to share some of the same values. But this also allows for conflicting opposites within each of the four temperament types. It makes the mix even more mixed up and confusing. But now you know how it all works. Hopefully this information will simplify the complicated.

Let's look at how this great subdivide affects one of the basic temperaments. This is just for a demonstration, not an in-depth analysis.

Let's use the amiables as our example.

The amiables have qualities that are formed from how they experience life and how they focus their attention. As you may recall, we called them inner-feelers with the motto: *Does it help someone?* Their contribution to quality is the ability to be empathic. This being true, they are best suited for a job or profession that requires and rewards these attributes.

When you review the page that follows for some suitable professions/jobs, you'll see that the ones for amiables all directly help their fellow human beings directly and personally. Now factor in these two new dualities and you can further subgroup the amiables into positions that require specific traits in how they achieve their goals of helping people.

Authoritative amiables bring to the table the ability to help people by being responsible and accountable, being able to work within structured guidelines. Suitable professions for them are nurses, librarians, private secretaries, and so forth.

On the other hand, impulsive amiables work best in environments with less structure and more freedom to do what they want from moment to moment. They respond well in decorative design, the arts, music, food preparation, and anything that deals with any of our senses.

Adaptive amiables love to create a better, happier future for others, but they are very flexible in how they do so. Ideal professions for them are the ministry, social work, tutoring, etc.

Strategic amiables seek to help move people in structured ways that create a preferred future for them. Natural professions for them are counselors, therapists, and psychiatrists.

And the same pattern holds true for each of the other three basic temperaments and their subgroups. Altogether, it's a grand and wonderful plan that explains so much of who we are and who they are. It plainly illustrates how we differ and complement each other, as well as which professions or jobs suit us best.

The Magic of Sixteen

It is well known by physicists that everything physical in this world is made up of atoms and their subatomic particles. Elaborate experiments have proven that an atom can be broken down into these subatomic particles, which are the building blocks for the atom and ultimately all matter. It may be a coincidence (or not) that the standard model of elementary particles consists of sixteen different types. Not being a physicist, I can't make any bold statements about the similarities. But I do think that this is more than just interesting.

Which of the sixteen groups in the great subdivide are you? Your spouse? Your family? Your friends? Your associates? Anyone else in your life? What kind of profession/job is right for you?

The charts on the following pages could prove helpful for making your determinations. The first one is really a chart of the values that are inherent within each of the sixteen types. These are values that will most likely persist throughout life. These are the defining values that genetically create who we are.

CHARACTERISTICS OF THE 16 T-CODE TYPES

	AMIABLES	FEELERS	EXPRESSIVES	
	Adaptive	**Impulsive**	**Adaptive**	**Impulsive**

	Adaptive	**Impulsive**	**Adaptive**	**Impulsive**
	INFP 3% • Skilled with people • Caring, empathetic • Deep relationships • Tuned into emotions of others • A peacekeeper • Perfectionist	**ISFP 10%** • Hates routine • Values freedom • Values pleasure • Creativity & variety • Sensual experiences • Flexible • A free spirit	**ENFP 2- 3%** • Values ethics • High morals • A need for empathetic relationships • Human satisfaction comes first and performance second	**ESFP 10%** • Seeks fun & action • Lives in the present • Loves spontaneity pleasure • Kind to people • Reacts emotionally • Natural negotiator
	Strategic	**Authoritative**	**Strategic**	**Authoritative**
	INFJ 2-3% • People focused • Caring • High need for stability • Hard workers • Determined • Single-minded concentration	**ISFJ 10%** • Dedicated worker • Dependable • Team player • Protective • Sees to others' security • Will work long hours on thankless jobs	**ENFJ 2- 3%** • Developer of people • Responsive and reliable • Educator • Outgoing and expressive • Charismatic • Sociable & popular	**ESFJ 10%** • Can talk to anybody • Outgoing • Tells and directs others • Tradition important • Warm hearted • Strong value systems
	Adaptive	**Impulsive**	**Adaptive**	**Impulsive**
	INTP 3% • Values theory & insight • Prefers to work alone for the group • Lives in a world of ideas • Reserved • Impersonal	**ISTP 10%** • Master of tools and instrumentation • Enjoys risk that goes with change • Soft-spoken • A loner	**ENTP 2- 3%** • Values theoretical insight & logic • Tends to overlook human element • Task oriented • A creative thinker	**ESTP 10%** • Craves excitement & action • Likes living on the edge • Great w/challenges • Can be demanding • Fun loving • Highly observant
	Strategic	**Authoritative**	**Strategic**	**Authoritative**
	INTJ 1% • An original thinker • High achiever • Future focused • Single-minded when concentrating • Unimpressed with authority	**ISTJ 10%** • Task oriented • Serious and quiet • Responsible, careful • High need for rules and security • Sees job through to the end	**ENTJ 2- 3%** • High self image • A natural leader • Can be arrogant • Inflated confidence • Future oriented • Frank & decisive • Will not follow	**ESTJ 10%** • High economic need • Controlling, impatient • Gets things done • Insensitive • Practical & realistic • No time to waste • A natural for business

INNERS (left margin)

OUTERS (right margin)

ANALYTICALS	THINKERS	DRIVERS

MOST FITTING POSITIONS/JOBS FOR EACH TYPE

	AMIABLES	**FEELERS**	EXPRESSIVES	
	Adaptive	**Impulsive**	**Adaptive**	**Impulsive**
INNERS	**INFP 3%** • Ministry • Missionary • Social worker • Library research • Tutoring • Child Counseling • Humanities • Language	**ISFP 10%** • Decorative design • Purchasing • Nursing • Teacher • Forestry • Landscape design • Gardening • Art and Music	**ENFP 2-3%** • Teacher • Minister • Communication Arts • Journalist • Orator • Novelist • Screenwriter • Playwright	**ESFP 10%** • Real estate agent • Business • Sales • Elementary teacher • Social worker • Actor or Actress • Advertising
	Strategic	**Authoritative**	**Strategic**	**Authoritative**
	INFJ 2-3% • Counselor • Therapist • Psychology • Psychiatry • Music and Art • Public relations • Human relations	**ISFJ 10%** • Homemaker • Registered nurse • Practical nurse • Librarian • Private secretary • Curator • Middle management	**ENFJ 2-3%** • Teacher • Sales • Media • Ministry • Therapist • Executives • Primary care physician	**ESFJ 10%** • Service occupations • Teacher • Clergy • Coach • Sales rep • Supervisor
	Adaptive	**Impulsive**	**Adaptive**	**Impulsive**
	INTP 3% • Architect • Logician • Mathematician • Scientist • Technologist • Tech teacher	**ISTP 10%** • Trades person • Carpenter • Mechanic • Plumber • Surgeon • Pilot • Furniture maker	**ENTP 2-3%** • Entrepreneur • Teacher • Engineer • Business • Human relations • Problem solving positions	**ESTP 10%** • Administrator • Deal maker • Entrepreneur • Sales promoter • Defense lawyer • Industrialist • Real estate developer
	Strategic	**Authoritative**	**Strategic**	**Authoritative**

	INTJ 1%
	• Science
	• Technology
	• Scientific research
	• Executive
	• Human engineering
	  type positions
		ISTJ 10%
		• Librarian
		• Dentist
		• Bank examiner
		• Auditor
		• Accountant
		• Legal Secretary
		• Tax attorney
			ENTJ 2-3%
			• Military
			• Leader in almost any
			  profession
			• Science
			• Technology
			• Executive
			• Business
				ESTJ 10%
				• Corporate law
				• Politics
				• Police work
				• Military
				• Business
				• Supervisor

	ANALYTICALS	**THINKERS**	DRIVERS	**OUTERS**

The second chart places each type in the most fitting jobs or professions that are right for them. It doesn't mean that we have to follow this exactly, but it will give us a feel for the positions that use each individual's strengths.

These charts offer so much insight into the study of human nature. There, on a couple of pages, is the big picture of all humanity and our earthly purpose. Please take time to study where everyone fits and our interdependence on each other. If you can, try to see the picture that is painted here. Try to recognize the balance of our world that is presented for you to understand. I think you will be a lot more tolerant of others after you spend a few minutes looking them over—and a lot more amazed by how beautifully crafted our earthly experience is. Your awareness of self should be kicked up a notch. You will note that the Myers-Briggs classifications and population percentages are listed for each of the sixteen types.

You can use these charts to find where you fit into the big picture. Look up on the Internet the Myers-Briggs classifications that seem to best describe you. There is a wealth of information out there to help you with your specific needs.

Also, check out how different the feelers and the thinkers are in their characteristics, and what they end up doing in their lives. Look at the divisions we have in our country, such as Republicans and Democrats, big business and labor, conservatives and liberals, religious and nonreligious, rule makers and rule breakers, and the list goes on and on. These divisions are nothing more than our temperaments and their values conflicting with other's inherent natures. Please grasp this concept; it is one of the most important lessons we can learn!

You might recognize that you are wasting your time trying to annihilate or overpower the other side that is in conflict with you. You might see that we have the possibility of working together for the common good. There are choices in front of us. With this kind of knowledge, we can all benefit.

Understanding temperaments is critical to understanding human nature. Ways of thinking, feeling, and acting, along with how we behave naturally is the definition of human nature. We have just learned the inner workings of the temperaments. Now we can more fully understand exactly how people are different and why they are different.

With this information, you can't help but become more tolerant of others who are not like you. Maybe someone will read this book and become more tolerant of you. Wouldn't that be nice?

With all these different dualities, it's no wonder it's all so difficult for us to understand. Our next poem tries to clarify this:

People are different in so many ways,
Figuring them out puts one's mind in a haze.
What is the grand purpose of us being opposing?
I have some ideas, but I'd just be supposing.

This duality thing has me all in distress.
It's all too confusing, I can truly confess.
I wish being human wasn't so complicated.
Will someone please get our nature translated?

The conflict in life comes from this simple equation.
Opposites in nature equals our human frustration.
This stage has been set for us actors here learning.
It's these mysteries of life that keep our minds churning.

Once we understand how this whole thing transpires,
Life becomes a blessing; it nourishes and inspires.
Our problems will guide us toward a greener pasture
We'll become more adept, and our lessons we'll master.

Lesson 8

To Thine Own Self Be True

I must first know myself, as the Delphian inscription says; to be curious about that which is not my concern, while I am still ignorant of my own self would be ridiculous.
—Plato, *Phaedrus*

Now that you realize that each of us is born with a basic temperament and you understand the value of each temperament in the grand scheme of life, there is a great lesson here. You can't help being who you are any more than they can help being who they are. As a matter of fact, each of us should embrace who we are.

"To thine own self be true" is excellent advice for dealing with others. It's also vital to living a satisfying, fulfilling, and productive life without driving yourself and others crazy. It is one of the first and most important steps in mastering human nature.

This might sound oversimplistic, but consider how much time, energy, and emotion is spent on trying to make others—and especially ourselves—into people we cannot be. This can lead to far-reaching negative consequences.

Do These Growing Pains Sound Familiar?

I remember my growing pains as a teenager—most of all the insecurity that probably all teens experience in varying degrees. It seemed like the guys who were the loudest, boldest, and funniest were the coolest, most liked, and most admired by the group. I wanted to be like them to satisfy my developing ego. It didn't work.

Try as I might, I never felt comfortable being like that. And I wasn't very good at it. It really bothered me that I wasn't the leader of my peers—and that others were always in the forefront. I especially envied those who were able to connect with the girls.

What I was going though was nothing more than what each and every teenager experiences.

As we are growing up, our beliefs and values are highly influenced by our peers. Our actions are often a result of the validation or invalidation we receive from them.

Scientists have found that self-esteem and self-confidence are closely linked to certain chemicals that are produced in our brains. Social validation actually increases the levels of serotonin and dopamine, which makes us feel good.

Conversely, lack of these chemicals can lead to depression, self-destructive behavior, and even suicide. Unfortunately, a teen's self-concept is almost entirely dependent upon external validation and peer judgment means almost everything to him or her. Sorry, parents; that's just the way it is.

There is much incongruity in how we see ourselves and how we perceive others' opinions of us. This can result in confusion of our self-esteem and our identity. But each of us at some point has to try to discover who we really are and forget about what everybody else tells us we should be or do. Finding oneself can be a difficult, traumatic, and overwhelming process for anyone.

Not knowing who you are or where you fit in and not being able to understand yourself and others have to be stressful and frustrating. Maybe you went through something like this as you were growing up. Or maybe it's been so long that you've forgotten what it was like. Probably not, since it is hard to forget—no matter how old we get.

It's a wonder any of us get through that time of our lives unscathed. If the truth of the matter were known, probably none of us really do. As a result, we all have scars and hurts that we carry with us, some of us for the rest of our lives.

Issues of poor self-esteem and lack of self-confidence can have their roots in our teen years. And as a result, we may develop insecurities that can keep us from developing to our full potential. Some lives are deeply affected by all this. Some people carry these issues all through their lives and never get over them. Poor self-esteem issues usually are a result of self-judgment.

God Takes Pity on Drunks and Fools.

In college, I joined one of the best fraternities—best in drinking, partying, and debauchery. One reason people drink, of course, is to lose their inhibitions (or limitations of their temperament) and be someone they're not for a few hours. I did a lot of partying for that reason; to be funnier, bolder, and louder. It's a miracle I lived through it all, but God takes pity on drunks and fools.

Even though I knew I wanted to be a dentist, I had developed a lack of self-confidence that kept me from excelling in my college studies. I had a fear of failing, which made it almost impossible for me to succeed.

So overpowering were the feelings that they almost immobilized me. The voice in my head kept telling me that there was no way I was ever going to make it. I listened to the voice, and I believed what it was telling me. I came very close to not even applying to dental school because I knew I probably wouldn't make it. I thought, *Why should I even bother trying?*

My fear of failing kept me from doing what I needed to do to succeed. If you really believe you can't do something, then you won't. And you will be proven right. I ended up partying way too much, and my grades suffered. You get the picture. Ralph Waldo Emerson said, "Fear defeats more people than any other one thing in the world." It almost did me!

It's easy to look back at this time in my life and see how my negative self-image and poor self-esteem kept me from doing my best. And in this competitive world, doing your best is mandatory for success. In analyzing why I had this negative and defeatist attitude, I have to attribute a lot of it to my underlying insecure feelings and thinking I wasn't as good as I thought I should be. I guess my serotonin and dopamine levels were too low because I felt a lack of validation from others.

How stupid is it to almost ruin your life because of your peer group's lack of approval? And even more idiotic—it was mostly due to the voice in my head. Thank God I did go ahead and apply to dental school. And thank God the dean of admissions had more faith in me than I did in myself.

My Future Success Hung by a Thread

Looking back, I'm sure an understanding of the T-Code would have saved me a lot of grief and inner turmoil. Maybe I could have seen why I was like I was and not been so frustrated in trying to win the approval of my peers. I might have understood that since my temperament type (strategic analytical) makes up only 1–2 percent of the population, I really was the odd man out. But maybe I would have also seen my strengths and become okay with it all. My children will get a good understanding of the T-Code and get a chance to know themselves and others before they go through what I did.

I cringe at the thought of what could have happened to me if I hadn't been accepted into dental school. It's rather scary. At the time, I knew there was no way I could get accepted into any professional school with the grades and test scores I had accumulated.

My life's path was mercifully determined by the actions of the head of admissions when he took my rejected dental school application and singlehandedly placed it into the accepted file, secretly overriding the decision of the rest of the admissions board. Success in life sometimes does hang by a thread.

Before I was accepted, I went to one of my college counselors for advice. He was being honest with me when he stated my chances of getting into dentistry were slim to none. He said that with my degree in biology, I should consider pharmaceutical sales. I almost vomited at the thought of doing something like that. It just wasn't me. I became even more immobilized at the thought of working at something I knew I wasn't cut out for.

When I received that letter of acceptance into dental school, I had a revelation that changed my self-image. From that moment on, I no longer had an esteem problem. I swore to myself that I would be the best I could be and never allow negative thinking to overwhelm me again. I went on to do quite well in dental school and the years that followed.

The lesson here is an obvious one. Don't let negative thoughts and low self-esteem demoralize and disable you—or your son or daughter! Do let the real power of positive thinking go to work for you to fulfill your promise in life—whatever it is! Don't give up on doing what you were born to do! Don't settle for anything less!

It is important to understand ourselves and try not to compare ourselves to others who have strengths (and weaknesses) that differ from ours?

It all starts with having respect in yourself and faith in your given abilities. Then, knowing that you have certain qualities and strengths that are valuable to others allows you to pursue your own pathway through life.

A wise old dog trainer once told me that you can't train a dog against its nature. He said dogs of each breed have certain traits that make them fit in certain environments. In other words, you can't turn a lapdog into a guard dog and vice-versa. A hunting breed won't do well in a small closed area. My wife and I made that very mistake when we purchased our first dog, a springer spaniel. We lived in a condo with very little space for the dog to run.

Although we loved the dog very much, he developed some very destructive habits and ended up tearing up our house. We tried everything, including obedience-training school, but nothing seemed to help. When our firstborn arrived, we were worried that the dog might harm our baby. Sure enough, our fears were confirmed when he jumped up and scratched our baby girl. We reluctantly knew it was time for the dog to go.

We gave him to a couple who had two acres of fenced-in yard with a pond. With other dogs to run, play, and swim with, he was in doggie heaven. Wouldn't it be better if all of us knew where we fit so we could find our own version of doggie heaven?

Doesn't it make sense to find out who our children really are so we don't unintentionally cause them pain by forcing them to be something they aren't or making them go into a career that's totally wrong for them? How many parents try to map out their child's future but totally neglect the fact that they might not be cut out for it? I've known quite a few.

The Costs of Being in the Wrong Job

A recent Gallup poll found that a whopping 70 percent of Americans either hate or are totally disengaged in their jobs. Are you kidding me? 70 percent? Those numbers are gut wrenching when you think about the ramifications. The poll surveyed 150,000 full-time and part-time workers to arrive at the percentages.

These disgruntled workers are not only bad for office morale; they're also bad for the economy. An estimated $450–550 billion is lost each year due to lack of productivity, missed days of work, and other reasons.

How does this affect their personal happiness and their home lives? It obviously doesn't enhance it in any way. The survey also showed that when management tries to make their employees happy by giving them perks, such as catered meals, Ping-Pong tables, nap rooms, and in-office massages, it does little to improve office morale.

Nothing can replace the innate desire to show up to work every day. The only way this can happen is if you are doing what you love to do. It can't happen any other way. This is a travesty in society. We are obviously not preparing ourselves and our children for one of the most important aspects of life.

Napoleon Hill interviewed and studied some of the nation's most successful leaders, businessmen, and entrepreneurs of the early 1900s. For more than twenty years, he studied the behaviors and habits of men like Henry Ford, Thomas Edison, Harvey Firestone, John D. Rockefeller, Woodrow Wilson, Andrew Carnegie, Theodore Roosevelt, Dr. Alexander Graham Bell, and many more influential and successful people of his time. He wanted to learn the real reasons these men were so successful so he could help others reach their potentials.

He also studied more than sixteen thousand people from all aspects of life, and from his questionnaires, many vital facts were gathered.

One of the many conclusions he arrived at was that 95 percent of the successful people were in vocations doing what they loved best. He said in his monumental work *Law of Success*, "One of the outstanding tragedies of this age of struggle and money madness is the fact that so few people are engaged in the effort which they like best." He felt that there was a great need to help everyone find their niches in the world's work, where both material prosperity and happiness in abundance could be found. He said, "It is doubtful whether a person could be a failure doing that which they liked best."

Unfortunately, his words of wisdom went unheard, and we still haven't recognized the importance of this idea.

There are a couple of reasons why this still is happening. The most important reasons have been discussed in this book while explaining the T-Code. We have yet to fully understand that everyone is born with certain strengths and weaknesses. We don't embrace the fact that each of us will fit better in certain positions than others. We haven't bought into the fact that each of us was put on this earth for a specific purpose. Another reason is that we seem to value making money over everything else. Jobs or professions are sometimes chosen because of the pay only.

We all have innate passions for certain things in life. What if we could make a living doing what we are passionate about? Few people are fortunate enough to be passionate about their occupation, but they are much happier in their lives than those stuck doing something they hate or are disinterested in.

How important is this? Finding yourself and utilizing your God-given talents has to be one of the most important tasks for human beings. If it is such an important task, why do we spend so little of our time and resources on it?

Many years ago, Confucius said, "Choose a job you love, and you will never have to work a day in your life." I think that Confucius was on the right track with his observations, but another factor has to be present to truly love your work. I believe you also have to have a purpose for working that is greater than self-gratification.

A Purpose for Living

As we will find out in later lessons, living just for our selfish desires will only take you so far in this world. Finding a purpose and a philosophy for living is imperative for a life that is meaningful and worthwhile. There is a next step from here that is just as important.

Having a purpose greater than your monetary needs is mandatory for self-fulfillment and is imperative for job satisfaction. Napoleon Hill also said, "Those who work for money alone are always underpaid, no matter how much they make." He believed the real rewards in life couldn't be measured in dollars alone. Having a chief definite aim and purpose in life was mandatory for happiness because you are doing what you were intended to do.

Living only for material success measured by a fat paycheck can be a recipe for discontent and personal dissatisfaction. Society places so much emphasis on having money to buy material possessions that we are missing out on some very important aspects of the rewards available to us in life. There are rewards much greater than money for us if we really knew the truth about human nature.

Making a difference in this world by helping and serving others has been said to be one of the keys to personal happiness. In a speech to the students of Silcoates School, Albert Schweitzer said, "I don't know what your destiny will be, but one thing I do know: the only ones among you who will really be happy are those who have sought and found how to serve others."

From *The Selected Writings of Ralph Waldo Emerson* comes one of the most descriptive and concise quotes ever written on this subject. "It is one of the beautiful compensations of this life that no man can sincerely try to help another without helping himself." A number of great thinkers throughout history seem to have come to the same conclusion; service to others is mandatory for a happy life.

These quotes are meant to help illustrate the fact that helping others in life in some way or fashion is so important to our own individual happiness. "To thine own self be true" doesn't mean that we become self-absorbed and only aware of how we fit into the big picture of life. That is a dead-end street that will lead us nowhere. We also have to help others along the way.

The Best Way To Be Successful with Those You Love

As I've told you, my wife loves excitement, stimulation, and spontaneity, yet she married a person who cannot give her all these things on a consistent basis. I just can't do it. It just isn't me. After years of beating her head against the proverbial brick wall, trying to get me to be someone I wasn't, she finally gave up and gave in. She now understands me and accepts me for who I am, and our marriage works so much better now because of it. I have learned to understand her and her needs. Therefore, I try my best to help her get what she wants.

I've learned the best way to be successful with people—especially your spouse and children—is to help them get what they really want. And what they want may not be what you want. (I'm not referring to materialistic items or advocating spoiling them, although I am 100 percent guilty of doing this.)

The whole system of human interaction is perfectly created for conflict, and a lot of times, it can be found at home. Conflict of interests within the family unit can sometimes escalate into the most devastating and traumatic experiences we can go through in our lives.

We have to learn to realize that these conflicts are exquisitely, divinely, and purposefully devised. But when we recognize this as a fact, we may be able to rise above it. But we need some help in order to do this.

Most of all, it begins with understanding yourself so you can be who you are. *To thine own self be true.* It continues with allowing others to be who they are so they can be true to themselves. Will there be conflict? Definitely! But maybe, just maybe, with this kind of knowledge, both of you can get what you want without a fight. And wouldn't that improve the quality of your life—and that of everybody around you? Will it be easy? No it won't. But it beats the alternative.

Our next summary poem tries to convey the message that it is so important to be yourself. Try to let go of wanting to be someone you aren't. *To thine own self be true*!

This is the end of the first half of this book. We have been learning so much about the makeup of the different types of people. We have come a long way in our understanding of our differences and opposing values that define us as pieces of the humanity puzzle. Congratulations! You now know more about people than ever before. This knowledge will be very useful in day-to-day life, and your communications with others will definitely be enhanced.

But there is still much more to learn. In the next part of the book, we will be uncovering more mysteries of human nature and revealing the secrets to mastering them. I promise you it will be enlightening and rewarding.

"To thine own self be true," he boldly proclaimed.
"Easy for you," in tears she explained.
"There's too much pressure to be so contrived."
"That makes me lose sight of what's really inside."

"Just be who you are," as he cut in to talk,
"It's simple to do; just walk your own walk."
"I don't even know how," she was quick to come back,
"Or where to begin, how to get back on track."

"The first thing you do," he retorted with passion,
"Is quiet your mind, in some way or some fashion."
"Open your heart and hear what it's saying,"
"Be sure that you listen without vacillating."

Whoever you are, and whatever you do,
Don't ever lose sight of the vision inside you.
There's nothing more special in life than this:
Is to be who you are and find your own bliss.

Part 2

A Path toward Mastery

Lesson 9

Points of View

You have your way. I have my way. As for the right way, the
correct way, the only way ... it does not exist.
—Friedrich Nietzsche, *Thus Spake Zarathustra*

Let's get down to some dirty work with this lesson because it might be a tough one to deal with. If everyone sees the world differently from each other, then who sees it the way it's supposed to be seen? Who is right? If you answer "yourself," then at least you are being honest.

Of course *your* perception is the right way, right? And why is this so? It's because your perception *becomes* and *is* your reality. What evidence do you have otherwise? And that is the problem right there. We only have a limited way to evaluate and judge the world.

We only have a certain capability, a certain set of internal tools to see, feel, evaluate, judge, and experience life. It is really difficult—if next to impossible—to see things from another's point of view because they have their own and different capabilities. We need to begin to see that we are all limited in our perception.

What if we begin to understand that what we see, perceive, and ultimately judge may not be all that there is? (Because it isn't.) Maybe there are different points of view that are valid. (Because there are.) Can we do it even if it means invalidating what you believe to be true? (Probably not.)

Do you think you can deal with this idea? Maybe on paper, but when push comes to shove, I bet you will continue to stand your ground in some fashion.

What Is the Real Truth?

When it comes to our differences in points of view, there is no universal or ultimate truth; we can only see a very small fragment of the total perspective. This last statement takes away our "right" to be "right." Maybe most of our "truths" that we hold so dear aren't really true. If your truth can be challenged by someone's opposite truth, then there is a good chance that there really isn't a truth here. It's probably but just a point of view.

Understanding that opposing truths exist because points of view differ is fundamental to mastering life! This is a very difficult concept to grasp. Life is a bit hazier when you start seeing the world like this. It is less concrete, not so absolute. It's kind of scary to begin to think this way. We all want our lives to be secure and stable. We want to be able to know what we are doing is right, and that we are right. So when there is ambiguity, there is also anxiety. And that is not a good feeling for us.

I have found that learning to live with ambiguity and uncertainty was necessary for me to become more open to different possibilities. Living with my wife and her feelings sure helped me with that lesson. Life becomes a lot more wondrous and amazing when you really comprehend that you don't comprehend life. When you start believing you have things figured out, then you act as an authority. When you know that you don't know, then you continue to act as a student. A true student is open to new lessons.

Maybe the best thing we can do is begin to recognize that what we see, feel, and believe may not be as real as we think. The only people who can be certain of anything are those with closed minds. Think about that for a while!

Everyone's point of view is different, like all possible views from a mountain. The view from the top of the mountain looks completely different than if you are at the bottom or from any point between. One view is just that: one view. It would be hard to argue that any one of those perspectives is wrong. But they are all different.

Einstein's theory of relativity can be applied directly to this concept. Everything is relative from the perspective of the observer. This idea changes everything if you really understand it.

That's how people see things so differently. They are at different places in life. They have different temperaments, different values, different brains, and completely different life experiences. Your individual point of view is created by the summation of all these things. What we perceive, how we perceive, and the way we process everything is individualistic.

What we are is revealed by our points of view. So much of our perspective is formed from the inherent values created by our genetic makeup.

I am slightly colorblind and can't see reds and greens as most everyone else can. I found out that I was colorblind when I had to have a comprehensive physical before going to dental school. So at the age of twenty-one, I found out that I had a minor disability. I was totally unaware of this before the physical. How could I have not known this?

Being slightly colorblind is really no big deal, but it illustrates how our internal equipment can limit how we perceive the world. My eyes can't be trained or fixed to see colors like others. There is no cure, medication, surgery, or solution for this problem. I can conceptually understand what I am missing, but I can't see the colors like most people do.

I think that we are all slightly "blind" in some form or fashion. We are just not aware of it yet, just as I was unaware of my colorblindness until the doctor informed me of it. Unfortunately, most of our shortcomings and deficiencies are not physical or mental; they are emotional. These are not as easy to point out or accept because of our emotional attachments to our perceptions.

Our points of view can never really be the same for a number of reasons. We can never exactly see things from another's point of view. We can try to get as close as possible, but our own perspectives will always get in the way.

> The only reality I can possibly know is the world as I perceive and experience
> at this moment. The only reality you can possibly know is the world as you
> perceive and experience at this moment, and the only certainty is those perceived
> realities are different. There are as many "real worlds" as there are people.
> —Carl Rogers, *A Way of Being*

We have been over and over how our God-given temperament helps create our preferences in thinking and feeling, and we also covered values and how different everyone's are. Then there is the final major factor in this equation that determines our perceptions and our points of view: the lives we are thrown into (our external environments). This is a huge creative force in our development as an individual. Everyone's life experiences are different, which helps create uniqueness in all of us.

Play the Hand You're Dealt.

We are all dealt different hands of cards on earth. Some of us have been very fortunate and have it better than others. Some have been blessed with one or more positive attributes, such as looks, brains, money, status, health, talent, location, culture, parents, family, luck, or personality. And then there are those who had a very difficult life without the benefits of many or all of these gifts. How do these attributes help shape our selves?

Do the people who were given the most by birthright end up being the most successful and having the happiest lives? I think you know the answer to that one. Why is it that some people who have had the most difficult backgrounds end up overcoming it all and excelling in their lives?

Why do some people learn valuable lessons that make them stronger and wiser while others never learn and are doomed to repeat the same problems? Those are questions I'll attempt to answer as we get deeper into the more complicated human nature issues.

According to ancient Chinese wisdom, two facets make up who we are. They believed that people were born with an innate temperament, which is what I have been talking about. They also believed that character is something we acquire during our earthly experiences. Our character reflects the intentions of our hearts.

They felt that positive character traits reflect the alignment of our temperament with our spirits, and negative traits are acquired when we are separated from our spirits.

They said that our innate temperament plus our earthly acquired character equaled our personalities. I think that is a pretty good summation of what makes us who we are. So even the ancients were aware of how important this information is. But what do our different perceptions mean to us in our daily lives? How can we benefit from this kind of knowledge? Is it really all that important?

Talking to a Teenager

Recognizing that we all have different points of view can impact our lives right in our own homes. Ever try to communicate with a teenager? Talk about different perspectives on life! This is "meat and potatoes" human nature material. This is the stuff that life is made of. Trying to talk to a teenager is representative of trying to talk with anyone who has a different perspective than you do. It's just plain difficult.

I have had the privilege of raising two wonderful children and have the battle scars to prove it. Just kidding. I have been very blessed and am very fortunate with the cards I have been dealt in this aspect of my life. But, there have been—and will continue to be—difficult and frustrating times when I attempt to communicate with them.

One of the most frustrating parts of being a parent is the fact that I have been through so much more than they have—so I can speak from experience when I try to help them with something—but they end up not listening to my magical words of wisdom.

I would love to be able to transfer all the lessons I have learned to my kids so they wouldn't make the same mistakes I have made. But that ain't gonna happen! And maybe it's not meant to happen that way for a reason.

We have different points of view that create how we see things and how we listen to things. A teenager's ability to listen to his or her parent's pontifications is limited by age, experience, values, interests, motivations, and the depth of the relationship with the parents. Our frustration comes from our inability to connect with them, and we feel helpless or angry. We might start yelling at them, which makes them shut us out even more.

I learned the hard way that what I would like to communicate to my kids is usually not even remotely interesting to them. And if it isn't interesting or beneficial to their perspective on life, then I am pretty much wasting time for both of us.

Communication, real communication, doesn't happen very often. I have to sometimes wait for the right opportunity to speak my peace. I have to try to get them to listen to me when it's a really important matter.

As parents, I think we all believe that what we say to our kids should be obeyed—just because we say so. How many times have we been guilty of saying, "Because I told you so!" when they question one of our commands? You may force them to do something, but it doesn't mean they understand the real message behind it. *You can lead a horse to water, but you can't make him drink.* We can't impose our will on them if there is no understanding or listening on their part.

There is also a fact that we either don't know or forget when it comes to understanding our teenagers. It has been proven that their brains are not yet fully developed. This means that their brains are simply not yet equipped to think things through. Maybe our own brains haven't fully developed yet. I can't wait until mine does!

Values and judgment can be learned, but you can't learn and use them if you don't have the necessary hardware. Our rational brains continue to develop into midlife. Insight, wisdom, and higher values come only after our brains are capable of processing this kind of information. This explains how our values change as we mature. It's an actual brain change!

Dr. Lawrence Steinberg, a developmental psychologist, has done some groundbreaking research on teenagers' brains and the way they function. Using neuroscience and new brain-imaging techniques, he found that the part of the brain that is responsible for controlling impulsive behavior develops slower than other parts. He also found that certain incentive-processing centers in teens' brains become more sensitive right after puberty. They experience much more pleasure out of positive rewards.

They have difficulty weighing the risk-to-reward ratio than a more mature mind would have no problem assessing. So not only do they have an immature brain that isn't wired for logical and rational judgment, they also experience more pleasure from risky behavior than adults do. What a great combination for doing some really stupid stuff. Sounds pretty much like the way I was when I was a teenager!

The lessons to be learned here by parents are profound. First of all, we cannot always expect mature behavior out of our teens. We also have to understand that teens are motivated by pleasure and positive rewards—not the negative reinforcement that most of us usually give them. Telling them that something bad will happen if they do or don't do something isn't going to be as effective as telling them that certain positive rewards will be available if they do or don't do something.

We have to be more positive in our communication with our teens. But we tend to dwell on the negative a lot of the time, don't we? Being positive is a much better way of being, don't you think? It sounds like they can be our teachers—if we let them.

I believe the most important part of parenting is establishing and maintaining good relationships with your kids. Understanding their wants and needs without too much judgment is first and foremost.

Even when they do something ridiculous, it's critical that we aren't too hard on them. Their job as children is to make mistakes and learn from them. They have a difficult time understanding who they are and what they are supposed to be doing. A lot of the time, all we achieve as parents is making their development more difficult when we try to micromanage their lives. If we could just learn that making mistakes is crucial for learning, we might not be so emotionally charged and make bad situations even worse.

Dealing with Your Spouse

This is one of the hardest and most important of all the challenges we face as humans. Marriage is our greatest classroom for personal development. There is no hiding or escaping who you are with all your limitations and defects. Your interaction with your spouse will expose your true self and create many opportunities to experience all that life has to offer, both good and bad. I suppose our divorce rate is a good indicator of just how difficult it is.

I have shared my trials and tribulations within my marriage so you know what lessons I have had in this department, but I would like to ask you how you deal with a situation when there is a mutually important, emotional issue that you and your spouse see from different perspectives. This is a classic disagreement in action. Your options are:

- Fight about it until one gives in and is declared the loser (creates hard feelings on the loser's side).
- Overpower the other with the threat of fighting. This works well if you have already achieved dominance in previous fighting experiences (more hard feelings).
- Avoid the confrontation altogether and try to pretend it isn't important (creates a void and separation that could be damaging).
- Compromise where both kind of "win" and kind of "lose" (a draw).
- Give one his or her way with the stipulation that the other will get his or her way the next time (could be a satisfactory result for both).
- Try to find a way that allows both to feel good about the results. Discuss each of your points of view without judgment. (This is best if possible.)

How does it work in your relationship? Which side are you on usually? How does it feel when you are a winner or a loser? When your spouse has a different view on a critical issue, such as style of parenting, how do you handle it? Conflict resolution in a marriage is one of the most important ways to make or break it. Remember how quality works with both sides being creative forces? What if our marriage truly was based on this concept?

This is true in all human interactions. American folk singer Arlo Guthrie gave us a pathway to follow when he said, "Everyone has a responsibility to not only tolerate another's point of view, but to also accept it eagerly as a challenge to your own understanding. And to express those challenges in terms of serving other people."

I think Arlo was telling us to find a way to help the other person get what they want, not just try to beat them. Relationships are so much easier and satisfying when you can approach them in this fashion. This becomes easier when you are not so fixed in your point of view—and you know that you don't know it all.

This summary poem tries to explain our lesson with a classic argument:

"My way is the right way; your way is wrong.
Why must you argue your case so strong?
I've done my homework, why haven't you?
I've got the figures and facts to construe."

"There's no logic in your feelings; they really aren't real.
Your emotions are blocking me from your appeal.
How many times must we argue so long?
My way is right, your way is wrong!"

"Your way is wrong, my way is right (right brain).
Talking with you always ends in a fight.
It's easy to see you are out in left field (left brain).
Your stupid way of thinking has put up a shield."

"You never see things the way that I do.
My feelings get hurt all the time by you.
When will we ever get our lives straight?
There's a fine line here between our love and our hate."

Lesson 10

Breaking out of the Box

"To be or not to be?" That is not the question. What is the question? The question is not one of being, but of becoming. "To become more or not to become more?" This is the question faced by each intelligence in this universe.
—Truman G. Madsen, *Eternal Man*

This lesson will begin to explore something that is unique to human beings. Being human is having the potential to become more than we are presently. We don't have to be stuck in whatever situation we might find ourselves in at the present moment. We can change our lives if we choose. We can change ourselves from human beings to "human becomings." This choice allows us to grow, change, transform, and evolve.

A human being can be someone who just goes through life doing what his or her genetic instincts and reactions tell them to do. A "human becoming" makes the conscious decision to take control over his or her actions and overcomes natural limitations. We all have incredible potential if we make this choice.

The main prerequisite for us to begin to move in the direction of our potential is for us to start looking at ourselves a little differently than we presently do. To see ourselves in a more objective light is the main reason for this discussion. How to do this is one of the biggest obstacles faced by humankind. Let's try to tackle this issue by understanding some basics of human nature.

Each of us—with a predetermined temperament—brings inherent values and strengths to the table of life. But because we are who we are, we aren't somebody else of a different temperament with his or her inherent values and strengths, as much as we might want to be. On top of that, each temperament has its own built-in set of weaknesses or limitations.

Of course, that may seem totally obvious. Well, we might recognize this with our minds, but our egos and emotions can get in the way. As a general rule, our egos (the sense of self) proclaim us to be the center of the universe. It's a totally human tendency to overlook our personal errors, weaknesses, and limitations. And, often as not, we blame others for our inadequacies.

Hopefully, the T-Code allows us to see that we—and others—are not necessarily right or wrong in our conflicting views and ways. We just have different perspectives on things. And each of us brings our own piece of the puzzle to the game. It makes sense that we shouldn't be concentrating on who is right (ourselves usually) or who is wrong (them usually).

The real questions are: *What kind of results am I getting? How am I doing in my relationships? What kind of success am I having at work? How gratifying is it? Am I accomplishing good things in my life? Am I providing adequately for my family? And am I enjoying life, having my own kind of fun, and smelling the roses?* Important questions! And only we can answer them. What are your answers to these questions?

If things are not working in your life to your satisfaction, maybe you are stuck in your box, and the T-Code can help you find answers. And even if things are going well, they can always be better, right? Does that mean we have to become something we're not? Emphatically, no! But sometimes our egos keep us stuck in the box—to our detriment. That, in turn, can keep us from being effective in certain situations, especially when there's a conflict of temperaments.

Being "stuck in your box" can mean that you feel, think, and act today the same as you did yesterday and the days before. Basically, you are immobilized without any possibilities for different outcomes. You will be sentenced to a prison of your own making. You will react to life the same way over and over again. You have stopped learning and growing.

When you become emotionally attached to your point of view, you will close yourself off to other points of view. This poses a great danger to recognizing the truth when it appears. Nietzsche said, "Convictions are more dangerous enemies of truth than lies." He understood this concept.

How do you know if you are stuck in your box? Most of us live our lives relatively unconscious without too much self-examination. Socrates said, "The unexamined life is not worth living." Maybe that is a tad bit harsh and judgmental, but he raises a great point. He was trying to tell us to look at ourselves and step out of our unconsciousness. Questioning yourself and doing a little soul-searching is the first step toward recovery from this affliction. Becoming someone who isn't always so right about everything is the next step. I'm sure you have met others who are like this. It is easy to spot others, but it is a lot more difficult to recognize yourself as a know-it-all.

How Our Brains Work (or Don't Work)

When we are stuck in our box because of the ego's emotional attachments, there are actual processes going on in our brains that keep us from seeing things in a more objective light. There are specific neurons that respond to neurotransmitters, such as norepinephrine, that trigger a defensive state when we feel that our thoughts need to be protected from the influence or invalidation of others.

If we are challenged with an opposing and conflicting opinion, these neurotransmitting chemicals are released in the brain just as if your body was in danger of harm. In this defensive state, the primitive parts of our brains take over and override our rational thinking processes. Our emotions take charge, which causes us to remain our old narrow-minded selves.

Do you know defensive people that this describes? Of course! They are everywhere. The real question is whether you can see yourself being like this.

On a neural level, this defensive state is the same as when an animal is being attacked—even if the threat comes from a harmless opinion or facts that might be beneficial to our well-being. This keeps us from learning and growing.

Some people have made the decision that they aren't going to change for anything. They rationalize that they are comfortable with who they are, but in reality, they may just be very fearful of changing anything that has to do with their belief systems.

Unfortunately, when we become static, our brains become wired in such a way that we tend to become overly judgmental. We also tend to impose expectations on our selves, others, and life. We can only be happy when our expectations are met. (I don't know about you, but when I expect something to go a certain way, it usually doesn't.) The more emotional attachments you have to an expectation, the more discontent you can become when things don't go your way. Emotional ego attachments and expectations create most human suffering.

A Profound Question

We have already talked about being a know-it-all and how that affects us—and others around us. Let's look at this item from a slightly different angle. Someone once asked me a profound question: *Do you want to be right all the time—or do you want to be happy?* Now that's a good question. Think about it. Being right also means that anyone who doesn't see things your way is wrong. This is a great source of conflict that upsets people.

How often do we get uptight and suffer needlessly (or someone else does) over something totally stupid and thoroughly meaningless when it blows up into an argument? Why do we spend so much energy doing this? Why are we willing to put our relationships at risk over something that's basically trivial just to prove that we are right about it?

We are programmed to see things in certain ways, and then we feel obligated to defend our positions. Almost always in these kinds of battles, somebody wins, and somebody else loses. And more often than not, that somebody else is near and dear to you.

After many of these encounters I have thought, *Man, oh man. I wish I had just kept my big mouth shut. That sure wasn't worth arguing over and getting everybody so upset!*

But do we learn from our mistakes? We might learn something in the short term, but the next time something like this occurs, our egos take control again—and history repeats itself. What's going on here? On one side, you and your ego are totally convinced you are right. On the other, your opponent (and his or her ego) of a different temperament is just as sure he/she is right. And from each point of view and perspective, both might be right.

Being stuck in our boxes keeps us doing the same thing in the same way without ever questioning it. Sometimes we are so consumed with what we are doing we miss out on some very important aspects of life. We may become so focused on our desires that we can't see the big picture. One example is the classic workaholic. We all know people whose main function in life is work. They live to work, and they get good results at their work, but other aspects of their lives suffer.

Nasty Old Scrooge Proves the Point

A classic and beloved story illustrates this point beautifully. Remember nasty old Scrooge and his faithful employee Bob Cratchit? Scrooge was obviously very rich in terms of money and very poor in terms of relationships. But until his revelation, as brought forth by the three ghosts, his focus was only on making money. He blatantly disregarded other aspects of life.

Scrooge's life was dramatically out of balance, and he was stuck in his money-making box. In T-Code terms, Scrooge was the exaggeration of a driver, and Cratchit was the epitome of an amiable. The dynamics of this type of relationship sets up the story line.

The overly assertive, insensitive, cold, money-hungry businessman takes advantage of the good-natured, kind, sweet, loyal employee and uses the sweat of poor, defenseless Bob to line his own pockets without any compassion or caring. I always wondered why Bob didn't tell Scrooge to shove it and go find a better job, but I guess the story wouldn't have been as good. In truth, Bob Cratchit was just as stuck in his amiable box as Scrooge was in his driver box because of his total lack of assertiveness. (My Mom always said, "You gotta lay down to be a rug.") But this interaction demonstrates how big business is looked down upon by people with opposing temperament types. Big business, by its very nature, is in conflict with those who by their inherent genetics put people first.

When Scrooge had his epiphany, his whole perspective changed, and those around him loved him for his newfound generosity and caring. Breaking out of his box not only saved his own life but also the life of Tiny Tim. It's a wonderful story that has delighted people for more than a hundred years. The message is clear for all you drivers. Begin to develop the ability to understand and care for the feelings of others. The rewards will amaze you.

Do not forget that anyone in any of the four temperaments can break out and learn lessons that can change our lives and the lives of those around us. How about one of those amiables getting the drive and ambition to succeed in a business of his or her own? Or an analytical trying to be somewhat entertaining and exciting in a way that might motivate another? Or how about an expressive learning to focus on detail-oriented things without talking all the while?

Scrooge was blessed with the visits of his three ghosts, which allowed him to see himself as he really was. We all have our own demons or ghosts; most of them are mistakes from the past, resulting from ego-driven temperament. I know I do. Wouldn't it be great if we could see them as clearly as Scrooge did and do something about what caused them in the first place? Unfortunately, the most common of all problems that affects all of humanity is our inability to see ourselves as we truly are. Maybe with the help of the T-Code, we can get a better glimpse.

What's Wrong With Them—or is it Us?

When I graduated from dental school, I teamed up with a classmate to open our first office. For the record, he was a driver and I was an analytical, (note that we are both thinkers). We had no business knowledge and fewer people and communication skills. Both of us were unmarried, and we had little understanding of women (who are mostly feelers).

We took great pride in our technical skills, but when it came to all the other things necessary to run a successful business, it was the blind leading the blind. We didn't have a clue about what we were getting ourselves into! Sadly, we had no business experience, and our dental school didn't offer any business training courses whatsoever. The only people we knew to help us were dental supply salesmen, and they readily took advantage of our ignorance and sold us everything they could.

We needed staff members to help us run the practice, so we set out into uncharted territory to hire women to work for us. Funny—or not so funny—things happened along the way. Because of our inexperience, our lack of business knowledge, our overwhelming bank debts, and our basic temperaments, we didn't have much success with our staff. We created lots of drama and trauma and hurt feelings because we constantly did things and said things they couldn't handle from their points of view.

My partner and I held staff meetings to discuss the problems we would invariably encounter. Our style was blunt, to the point, judgmental, and uncaring toward our female employees. This would lead to hurt feelings, and they would become defensive. We would get angry and frustrated.

Each side would become firmly stuck in its emotional, reactive box, and we usually resolved nothing. What a waste of time! After the dust settled, our call for another staff meeting would be met with more resistance. We obviously weren't getting the results we wanted.

They all ended up quitting on us when they couldn't take any more of our inadequacies. Of course, we figured we had hired the wrong women. Our solution was to hire the "right" ones. But the same thing happened with them. At year's end, we had seventeen W-2 tax forms on our desk to prove how lousy we had been as employers. And that was for only four positions.

We got the hint and began to improve our management skills. It's true; you really can learn more from failure than success. We had to learn out of necessity. Quitting wasn't an option because of our overwhelming debt. Debt has a way of enslaving you like nothing else.

Being your own boss is one of the best ways to clarify your weaknesses quickly. If you're an employee, you can always blame your boss for your problems, quit, and look for another boss to care for you. As an employer, success depends on overcoming your weaknesses, not running from them.

I learned a very valuable lesson that is critical for creating a happy, productive staff. When people express themselves and feel like their viewpoints are appreciated, their defense chemicals decrease in their brains. The dopamine neurotransmission activates the reward neurons, making them feel empowered. It is much nicer having empowered employees.

Anyone in any field of endeavor these days has to be able to break out of his or her box to successfully deal with all the different temperaments and conflicting values. For us, it was acquiring the ability to deal with others in a caring, compassionate manner. And that was a very difficult thing for people with our temperaments. A happy, team-oriented staff is essential for the success of any business.

Breaking out of the box can mean different things to different people. It can help us focus on personal development in areas that we may not have realized we needed help. It can help us reach our goals—whether we do it voluntarily or we are forced to do so.

The goal isn't to lose our identities; we want to fill in voids or expand into other areas to become more rounded and better people. And in the process, we will revisit and revise some of our old built-in prejudices and misconceptions. We will also develop a better understanding of and compassion for people different from us. There's no better way to let go of all that stuff that keeps us stuck in the box—and stuck in life. Who benefits most from all this? You know the answer to that one.

If you have figured out your temperament, it's enlightening to read about the strengths of your opposite type and speculate what you might become if you had some of their strengths. I always wanted to be more expressive when I was growing up, but that wasn't something I was comfortable being, so I wasn't. Having a really big ego made me desire to be the center of attention, but being somewhat introverted didn't allow that to happen. I bet most of us wish we had strengths we don't have. It's only normal. We will never become something we aren't, but by understanding others and appreciating what they bring to the table, we can begin to open up new possibilities for the present and future.

More Help from Napoleon Hill

Napoleon Hill was keenly aware of the concept of breaking out of your box. After years of studying the world's most successful people, he uncovered the secret formula that is necessary for those who want to accomplish great things in their lives. In his book *Law of Success* he laid out the framework of personal growth that he claimed was "the true philosophy upon all personal success is built." His book was written to help people to reach their full potential.

I read the book many times over many years ago and I have to give much credit to it for helping me grow and break out of my box. Over time I have recommended it to many of my friends and colleagues. One day I had an opportunity to lend my copy to a young man who was searching for his direction in life. I knew this book contained what he required to help him clarify what he needed to do with his life and how to do it. Our conversation about the book got me back in touch with what I had learned from it. That evening I kept thinking about the book because it had been a while since I had read it. I remembered that there were many lessons in the *Law of Success* but I couldn't recall any specifics. A thought flashed through my head. What a crazy coincidence it would be if there were sixteen lessons.

I ran to my computer to look it up and sure enough, the *Law of Success* was organized into sixteen principles. As I was reading through them it became clear to me that his principles mimicked the strengths of the sixteen temperament types that we have discussed with the T-Code. I quickly matched each of his principles with one of the temperament types. It all easily fell into place. It was uncanny but very validating of my thought process in writing this book. It was also validation of Napoleon Hill's work, not that he needed any.

Breaking out of your box requires much personal growth and an intention to become the best person you are capable of becoming. I highly recommend picking up a copy of his book and learning from this genius who was way ahead of his time.

Stuck in the Box

You're already aware that I had a lot of voids to fill in my professional and personal lives. Back then, I didn't have a clue how to handle feelings, and as a result, I had a very poor track record with my relationships with women. This wasn't surprising because, as we've pointed out, most women are feelers, and I was stuck in my strategic analytical thinkers box. It was only natural that I couldn't relate to them.

Perhaps it's hard to accept now, but I honestly believed women were not actually human. I thought they were only placed on earth as obstacles for men to overcome for personal growth. I'm serious! I viewed them as illogical and irrational. And I was convinced using logic and reason were the only proper ways to live. I was like Spock on Star Trek who didn't understand emotion, especially theirs!

Then I married a woman who was my direct opposite and had a will that was much stronger than mine. After surviving her boot camp, I began to see I had been wrong about a whole lot of things. I didn't set out to view life in a totally different way, but because my wife was head of her class at the School of Assertiveness Training for Women, I began to see the light.

Being paired with someone who is your opposite in every way sets up some interesting learning situations. I believe divorce attorneys call them irreconcilable differences.

What are the repercussions of being stuck in our own boxes? Why can't we just stay where we are comfortable and keep doing what we are doing now? Why do we have to do grow and change?

Life is kind of funny when you try to do your own thing. Life has a way of pushing you and knocking you off center if you get too complacent. At least I have found it to be like that. If you don't solve a particular life problem, it seems to have a way of reoccurring until you do solve it. And you can't solve it without some personal growth or change.

If you start looking at life as a growth process, problems start to look like they are there for a reason. It's easier to see when you look back on how significant problems have shaped you and your life. You might get a little philosophical about life rather than choosing to be a victim of your circumstances.

As I have pointed out with my marriage and my business experiences, most—if not all—my problems have led me (or forced me) to change and see life differently. If I hadn't changed or grown, I would not have been married long and my business would have floundered or folded. I can flat-out guarantee that.

I highly recommend looking at your box and asking yourself if you are stuck or not. What kind of problems are you having in your life? Are they problems that will lead you out of your comfortable life and force you to take on becoming more than you are now? Look closely to see if this is true for you. If you don't change and grow, what will your life end up looking like?

A Sad Story That's All Too True

Something happened in my family that relates directly to this subject. My father-in-law passed away a few years ago, and it was very difficult for my wife to handle because they were so close in so many ways. The death of a loved one sure puts life into a different perspective. Many questions are asked. *Where is he now*? *Do you think he is aware of us in some way*? *Does he miss me as much as I miss him*? There are no answers. Only tears.

She was well aware of this lesson on breaking out of the box, and as we talked about her dad, she said he was an ideal example of a person who never accomplished it. He had so much potential, according to her, but he never fulfilled that promise. His enormous ego would not allow him to bow to anything or anybody, and he never admitted to being wrong.

He was willing to go to battle over every little thing, and he never gave in. No one was going to tell him what to do. He never learned some of life's most valuable lessons, and the results were sad indeed. Unfortunately, his own father had died before he was old enough to even remember him, and he grew up with little or no discipline. Priding himself on being a tough guy, he enjoyed getting into fistfights to prove it. He was a heavy drinker and lived a hard life, and as a result, his liver failed him in the end.

While he was still in good health, his routine was selling cars, hitting bars, and womanizing. As he grew older, the fighting slacked off, but he continued to get into arguments with family, friends, and employers. Although he was a very good salesman, he never kept a job for long. One by one, his friends and family members disappeared from his life until he was left with only his faithful daughter. He ended up in a small apartment with barely enough money to pay for necessities. His daily routine was watching TV until my wife picked him up and took him out to lunch.

It was a sad, sad way to end his life—stuck in an apartment the size of a box with his life stuck in a box of his own making. Only on his deathbed did he show any remorse, regretting some of the bad things he had done to others.

And then he was gone.

> "The greatest of faults, I should say, is to be conscious of none."
> —Thomas Carlyle, *The Hero as Prophet*

Our next poem was inspired by my father-in-law and how he might have viewed this subject, especially his relationship with women. I think we all have a little bit of this type of thinking in us (but hopefully not too much).

I'm comfortable who I am, so I'm going to hold fast.
I'm not going to change and invalidate my past.
All other people have to accept me as I am.
I ain't giving in; that's not part of my plan.

I don't care if you think I'm stupid or insane.
I'm my own person, and there I'll remain.
You have no effect on my feeling or thought.
Don't tell me what I should. Don't tell me what I ought.

It's not me with the problem; I know that it's you.
My way makes sense, no way to misconstrue.
But I'm not really pleased that we argue and fight.
And I'm feeling quite lonely; can you stay for the night?

Oh well, no problem, get on and get going,
I'll be just fine by myself, here on my own.
I don't need you or nobody right now.
I ain't changing me, no way or no how.

Lesson 11

The Mystery of Our Minds (Recognizing the Ego)

Once I rose above the noise and confusion
Just to get a glimpse beyond this illusion
—Kansas, *Carry On Wayward Son*

We are about to open a sacred vault that holds the hidden and treasured answers to some of the major mysteries of human nature. Within this special inner sanctum, we will spend the remainder of our time trying to learn one of the ultimate lessons of being human.

We had to first travel to the mountaintop where we could get the full view of our vast world and the expanse of humanity in order to grasp what we will find in this secret hiding place. Our new knowledge of temperaments, values, points of view, duality, and conflict will help create the background for what's next.

Although this information has been available for thousands of years and has been recorded by numerous cultures worldwide, only a privileged few have learned to master these secrets. The answers to these mysteries have been recorded in a way that has been very difficult to decipher. This "classified intelligence" has been kept away from us for a strategic reason.

It is not an understatement that this information is the most important worldly lesson we can learn as human beings. Here is where we begin the most advanced work of our course. This part of our study is the most important and the most difficult to grasp. This mystery is so hard to master because learning it goes against some of our most basic survival instincts.

Because it is so difficult to grasp, please be patient and do everything you can to be open to this material. I promise that there is a pot of gold at the end of your rainbow. Your golden reward will be the life you desire and deserve.

In order to begin to assimilate this valuable material, we need to agree that being human is very complicated and confusing. We all have the capacity for a broad range of emotions—from unbearable sorrow to overwhelming joy. Humans are capable of performing miraculous acts of compassion and caring, unspeakable acts of cruelty and savagery, and everything in between. How is this possible?

The enigma of human nature lies in the fact that humans are so incredibly and mysteriously diverse in the ways they think, feel, and behave. Up until now, the solution to this puzzle has been beyond comprehension.

This last mystery of human nature is difficult to explain, and it remains totally obscure to most of us. An analogy of our predicament would be like trying to explain what water is to a fish. If you were a fish and hadn't ever been out of the water, how would you know what air was? And if you had never experienced air, you couldn't really fully recognize the qualities of the water. We're back to the duality thing again.

Remember that we can only understand something when we can compare and contrast it to its opposite. The task at hand is to be able to explain in simple terms what lies beyond our "water" to make the "air" easy to understand. I will try my hardest.

The Duality of the Mind

We have learned how duality has shaped our temperament, our world, our perception, and our values. In other words, it has shaped everything we can sense. This will be the last duality we need to understand in this work. Our earlier exploration of duality is the foundation for grasping this new information.

This is the ultimate duality that defines all of us. It is so important, yet so misunderstood. This duality holds the answer to most of the problems we experience. This is the duality of the mind. This duality is something that most of us are not even aware of. It is the duality of the ego and the higher self. This lesson will describe the ego in full detail. The next lesson will concentrate on describing the higher self. This information can change your life!

A Native American legend helps us understand what we will be discussing.

An old Cherokee shaman was telling his grandson about a battle waging within people. He said, "My son, the battle is between two wolves inside us all. One is an evil wolf filled with anger, envy, sorrow, greed, self-pity, guilt, resentment, lies, false pride, and superiority. The other wolf is the good wolf, and it is full of joy, peace, love, hope, serenity, humility, empathy, generosity, truth, compassion, and faith."

The boy took this in for a few minutes and then asked, "Which wolf do you think will win?"

The old Cherokee man replied simply, "The one you feed."

Part of the mind, the "evil wolf," is the source of most of the conflicts we have in this world. With our different temperaments, our different values, and our different points of view, we are born to conflict with others. How we handle our conflicts is indicative of which wolf we are feeding, and this is the pathway to higher levels of being. Which source we choose for our emotions and behaviors makes all the difference in the world.

Before we get too deep into this subject, let me share my first recollection of becoming aware of the first part of our duality.

The Self is the Real Problem

When I was a kid, I used to love baseball. I followed the Saint Louis Cardinals like I was a part of the club. I would listen to every game I could with my dad on his transistor radio, and I would read every article about them in the Saint Louis *Post-Dispatch*. I remember reading an article in that paper about something that really confused me. It was about baseball, but it was not about the Cardinals.

The author was describing Japanese baseball teams and how they were so different from their American counterparts. He wrote that the Japanese would train much longer and harder. Individual success wasn't their top motivation. They placed the team's success above their own. They truly believed that being selfless was a prerequisite for being part of an organization.

I had a hard time understanding that concept. It really didn't compute in my brain how that would work. What is more important than *me* as an individual? From my perspective, my needs came before everything else in the world. How could anyone feel any different? That article and my inability to process that information have stuck with me for more than forty years.

Our culture has a hard time with this selfless concept. Somewhere along the line, the self became the top of the food chain. It's the only thing that matters, which is the source of most of our problems. The self is the evil wolf.

The concept of self is deeply embedded in our culture. Rugged individualism founded this nation and made it as it is today. We celebrate the achievement of the individual and the competitive rise to the top in every field of endeavor. The most visible people in society are the ones who are most successful in sports, entertainment, TV, film, and politics. We adore and adulate the people who have made it to the top.

We would love to be like them and receive the fame and fortunes they have. It seems that celebrities have become a godhead for us to worship. Is it healthy to place so much emphasis on these people? I think you know the answer to this one.

In order to understand why we have gotten to this place, we have to become aware of something very important. In the *Pogo* comic strip, we find a most profound observation and illustration: *We have met the enemy ... and he is us!* The real source of our problems lies within each of us. Fortunately, so do our solutions.

The Ego Mind (the Lower Self)

The first part of the mind's duality is what we refer to as the self, which we will call the ego. The ego is the supreme sense of self. We consider it to be consciousness, self-awareness, and self-perception. It's who we are in relationship to the world. We see ourselves as separate and independent from everyone else. It's "me against the rest of the world." It is also grounded in the lower, more primitive parts of our brains.

Since we see ourselves as separate, then we should put ourselves first and foremost. The ego sees itself as completely on its own, which is a very scary thought and a source of much fear. In order to feel comfortable we tend to unite with others who validate us because there is more security and power in numbers. The ego is very insecure because it has no solid foundation. It is built upon nothing that will last or prevail over time.

Learning the ego's ways is imperative for us to be able to get it under control. We must first learn just what the ego does, how it does it, and why.

The ego perceives everything with a comparison and a judgment. It literally lives by comparison. It has been said that the source of all unhappiness comes from our comparisons. How profound is this? After pondering this idea for a good length of time, I wholeheartedly agree! Next time you are unhappy, try and apply this concept to your situation.

We judge with good or bad, more or less, right or wrong, yes or no comparisons. And we believe we are perfectly correct in our judgments. Our judgments all come from our individual perspective and point of view, which we believe to be correct.

One of the main goals of the ego mind is to "get." The ego wants what it wants, when it wants it. To the ego, to give anything implies that you will have to do without it. Because of our basic insecurities, which are formed from the idea that we are on our own, we believe we have to get "things" to prop us up.

Things can be anything from material possessions, fame, fortune, power, relationships, and prestige—anything we can use to prove to ourselves that we are better than those who don't have them. We need to get things to prove our worth and to get some semblance of self-esteem. These things can become the driving force in our lives.

Even when the ego gives something, it's really trying to get something in return. A lot of our so-called good works are nothing more than our egos trying to look good in comparison to others—or trying to get something in return. It's a giving with ego strings attached.

Looking good is another main objective for our ego. If we don't look good in front of other egos (who will for sure judge us), then our self-esteem is damaged. How much we care about looking good is a good indication of the ego's dominance. How much of your energy is spent trying to look good? This holds true not only with our physical appearance but also in what we say and do and our possessions.

The ego also tries to gain praise and recognition from other egos in order to feel good about itself. It will use almost any situation to get those things from others in order to overcome its doubts.

One of the best ways to feel good is to become superior to another ego in some way. The ego will go to great lengths to get what it thinks it needs in order to build itself up—even if it means hurting another to get it.

In our society, we have created an almost endless variety of competitions that allow for winning egos to achieve some type of superiority over another. To the victor go the spoils. Unfortunately, it also creates a bunch of losers who are left in the dust.

Sports are a great example, and they are all about egos trying to beat other egos for superiority in a game that usually involves a ball of some kind. And our society rewards these ego ballgame winners to an incredible extent. This is a result of our worship of the ego.

Clash of the Egos

Egos can clash in any situation. Read that again! Any time and every time egos get together, it is an opportunity for some sort of competition. It makes for great reality TV shows, and many of them use the ego clash format. There is no need to script these shows since conflict will show up in any situation. It's really a pretty cheap and easy way to create a show. It seems that we as a culture like to watch other egos clash and fight. I guess it makes us feel better about ourselves when we watch others go at it. They fail to control themselves, a big fight breaks out, and they all end up looking like fools. We would never do what they are doing, would we?

How do we handle conflict? Our choices include getting angry, getting defensive, arguing, internalizing anger, fighting, avoiding it at all costs, and everything in between. Sometimes we do things in anger that we never thought we were capable of doing. When pushed to our limit who knows what we might do.

The natural instinctive reaction is to get upset and angry when someone wrongs us. It is unnatural and requires much restraint to hold back. Biting one's tongue isn't easy. Not jumping into the fire when an argument pops up isn't easy. We may feel that the other person is getting the upper hand on us when we don't defend ourself. We may even feel that it is a sign of weakness to not fight back. How about when something happens, someone says something, or someone says something back? It's off to the races. Now, World War III has started, and it's too late to turn back.

Does conflict from our differences in opinion always have to end badly? Obviously, it doesn't. Remember our other option: *Blessed are the peacemakers.* Do you personally know any peacemakers? There are not too many of them hanging around, especially when we need them. We have choices in our conflict issues, but we need to understand them thoroughly. There is something special about conflict that we have failed to grasp.

Conflict is a test that reveals the source of our actions! How we handle our conflicts is the litmus test for where we are presently with our personal growth. Which wolf are you feeding?

The Control of the Ego

The concept of the ego is difficult to explain, and it is also difficult to let go of the ego's control over us even if we do understand it. Just as an animal has survival instincts, so does the ego. One of the ego's main characteristics is a strong survival instinct that keeps it securely in place. Giving up control is like suicide.

Most of the ego appears to be located in the lower parts of the brain. These include the brain stem, which is the reptilian brain we talked about already, and the limbic system, which is called the mammalian brain. It is responsible for most of our emotions. These two parts of the brain, which are the most primitive, collaborate to form the ego. The ego is impulsive, emotional, and defensive. Not by choice, but by instinct.

Our emotional attachments, with which we identify ourselves, have to be defended for the ego's survival. This is where conflict with other egos begins and it can escalate from there.

Another characteristic of the ego is its inability to see that it is capable of being wrong. It is right—and will always be right—based on its ability to perceive. We have discussed in detail how temperament, point of view, and values mix together to create how we interpret ourselves and the external world we interact with. By being right, the ego shuts down any possibility of bringing in additional information that might alter one's view. That helps keep us stuck in our boxes.

If this seems like normal and customary behavior, you are correct. Most everyday, normal people run their lives like this. For the most part, the world is run this way. It's just business as usual.

The Ego is in the House!

The ego's dominance over us is solidified by the fact that it speaks to us continuously in our heads in a never-ending conversation. The voice in our heads has us locked in as a captive audience. The commentary that keeps running in our minds is what we listen to all day long.

We believe the voice is ours. We think we are responsible for all the talking in our heads. If you think that the voice is you, here is a little experiment for you. Make it stop for a while. Try to take control of it. Can't do it, can you? Then whose voice is it if it isn't yours?

This is why we identify with our egos so much. It's all we hear! W-EGO is on the air 24-7. It is all about ego—all the time—with no commercial interruptions. What the ego tells us is usually critical, cynical, judgmental, negative, and totally self-serving. This keeps us from accessing the opposing duality of our minds.

These short descriptions of the ego barely scratch the surface of how it controls us. Learning the egos tricks is a lifelong discovery.

I have discussed in detail all the ego conflicts that arise from our competing and opposing temperaments, points of view, and values. Hopefully you will agree that most of our misunderstandings and conflicts in the world originate from this.

I have demonstrated that conflict between nations, factions within nations, spouses, family members, employees, employers, and everyday strangers have their beginnings here. It is no stretch to say that the results can be catastrophic—in wars, riots, suicides, murders, divorces, and untold heartache.

Sometimes, the results can be much more subtle, such as arguments, hard feelings, alienation of friends and family, depression, emptiness, anger, and unhappiness. These are the results of being driven by the ego.

We need to shake loose the total control the ego has upon us—and start accessing our higher selves. We need to create balance between them. The key is to understand when we are being controlled by our egos and to recognize the symptoms.

Here are some of the characteristics when our egos are in control.

Traits of the Ego and Lower Self

- being self-centered
- feeling victimized by circumstances
- anger, frustration, or stress
- impatience
- neurosis, fear of the future
- conflicts between wants and needs
- being judgmental
- holding grudges and resentments
- needing to be right and superior
- attachments to things
- trying to be in control
- having feelings hurt easily by others

When you see a list like this, it's easy to want to convince yourself how great you are in some of these departments. How you are, thusly, a superior human being. This proves that you are operating at a level that really doesn't need much improvement. It's everyone else who needs fixing.

Wait, not so fast! Beware of the tricks of your ego! Believe me, the ego rules. It takes much work to throw it off its throne. Don't believe a word it tells you. Tricks like this are commonly used to keep you under its spell.

Some temperaments are more laid back than others. This sometimes allows these people to appear better than others in some of these areas, such as not getting so visibly upset or being flamboyantly self-centered. It might be easy to believe that your inherent characteristics are just naturally superior to others who might be more demonstrative in these types of things.

One solution to this is to concentrate on the ego items you absolutely can't dispute that describe your behavior. Are you easily stressed or angered? Do your feelings get hurt easily? Becoming aware of the ego's control is the first step in overcoming it. It's a long journey from here.

Life is a process that needs time to unfold and develop. Relinquishing the ego's control won't happen overnight. We need to go through certain experiences in order to learn and grow.

We have to feel the pain of our mistakes so we can move through them and be done with them. If we try to jump ahead too far, too fast, and too soon, we won't fully grasp our lessons. Be patient, work at your own speed, and acknowledge where you are in your life.

The Results of Being Driven by the Ego

Do you enjoy being unhappy, or upset, or depressed? How about when you feel unmotivated, empty, unfulfilled, dissatisfied, anxious, fearful, or resentful? Of course you don't enjoy feeling any of these ways, but these are all symptoms of being overwhelmed by your ego.

Anytime you feel any of these negative emotions, you can thank your ego for feeling that way. You are fixated on not having something outside yourself that is missing. You haven't gotten something you think you need. Once again, the ego is all about getting.

The real kicker about the ego is that even if you get what you think you want and need, the ego will never be satisfied. Well, maybe for a little while, but not for long.

The ego is a cruel master that will never let up on its desire for getting more. Think about the billionaires in the world. Surely they have enough. What about celebrities? Does all their fame and fortune make them the happiest people in the world?

But it's never enough. There is no end point. There is no stopping the ego's insatiable desire for money, power, fame, or whatever else it wants.

Is this what we choose to allow our lives to be controlled by? Up until now, maybe we didn't know there was a choice. But it is a choice—and you will know the difference soon. Unless we develop beyond the ego self, we will remain subject to endless conflict, alienation, and suffering. It will show up in our relationships and our interactions with others. How big a part of our lives is this?

It is imperative to see that there is another part of being human that will open a larger dimension of our consciousness. Just remember how difficult, controlling and overpowering the ego is. It is a foe to be reckoned with. It is a lifelong struggle to deal with our egos. Good luck; it won't be easy.

Our summary poem takes on the ultimate challenge of being human—and recognizing and overcoming our egos:

Where to begin? It's overwhelming to explain,
This ego part of self, so exhausting to contain.
Its rule is total; it's not happy with a fraction.
It wants what it wants, best give it satisfaction.

"I'm the center of the universe," it tries to declare.
"But there are so many others who make this unfair.
Please cater to me, as I'm most imperative.
My desires need attention; I'll provide a clear narrative."

If you don't treat it right, it's willing to get tough.
When it gets what it wants, though, it's never enough.
There will never be a way for it to find joy.
There's not enough praise, enough love to employ.

So what is the answer to this relentless master?
Relinquish its control and prevent a disaster.
This has been suppressed throughout man's long history.
The answer to our problems is to mastery the mystery!

Lesson 12

The Mystery Continues (Discovering the Higher Self)

Human mistakes and inaccuracies are no less important than divinity. The human condition creates divinity in the higher self. Thus, it is very important to be human and not to shun or hate our humanity. The incredible process of being human allows for the higher self to acknowledge and extract divinity from one's trials and tribulations.
—Lena Lees, *The Living Word of Kuan Yin*

It is necessary to state that the goal is not to get rid of the ego entirely. We just need to establish a balance between it and the higher self. Our worldly experiences are based upon our willingness to be subject to the lessons of the ego that bring us all our pain and suffering.

Through these lessons, we can access our higher self to rise above them and grow. Embracing the duality between the ego and the higher self seems to be the ultimate key to mastering our humanness.

Becoming fully human requires us to honor both of these dualities equally. If we only concentrate on the ego's needs, we lose access to the higher self. If we only concentrate on the higher self, we can lose our vulnerability and the lessons associated with the lower self.

What is the Higher Self?

The higher self is in direct opposition to the lower ego self. It has eluded most human beings throughout history because the ego is so much in control of people's actions. We can't gain access to the higher self as long as we are totally ruled by the ego. And the world we are living in today is the world of the ego. Understanding this will help explain much of how the world works and why we presently have the problems we do.

Becoming aware of the mind's dual nature is one of the first steps toward uncovering the higher self and creating a balance with it and the ego. As with any duality, we can't understand and appreciate one without the other.

117

In order to access the higher self, one has to begin to relinquish the ego's total control. We will never annihilate the ego—and we can't—but we can loosen its grip. Albert Einstein gave us some more great advice when he said, "The true value of a human being can be found in the degree to which one has attained liberation from the self." The self is, of course, the ego.

The mantra of the ego is "getting." The higher self knows that it is more blessed to give than to receive. We have all heard this a million times, but now you know the power in this statement. True giving means you have risen above the ego's control.

You don't need to get things for your well-being. You can give without expecting reciprocation. Giving doesn't have to be material things. It can also mean giving your time, attention, caring, and compassion.

The higher self knows it is not the center of the universe, which is a preposterous idea to begin with. By not competing with all the other "centers of the universe," we can devote our energies to more important matters. This helps create a humbleness that others can recognize.

There is a feeling of unification with all beings because we are interconnected, and we are dependent upon each other. We spend so much of our lives competing with others that we can't even see that we are engaged in this silliness.

The higher self understands what the T-Code has illustrated—that we are all just pieces of this big puzzle. One of the most important aspects of this book is that it contains solid, tangible research that allows us to see the big picture of humanity and how we all fit into it. The T-Code contains proof that we are just bit players in this grand theater of life. By understanding how others see things differently, we can start believing that perception is limited. And because of that, we see that the ability to judge others is limited also. This opens doors for us to access the higher self.

From there, we can develop traits that will impact us—and others—in positive ways. Traits like tolerance, compassion, helpfulness, and generosity will attract others to you. Since you will not be trying to be better than others, the conflicts in your life will diminish dramatically. We can all use some of that! What would your life look like if you didn't enter into ego competitions?

The higher self doesn't need to prove its worth, and this is not from a stance of superiority. It knows that it is connected to something much greater than any one individual can be.

One of the main characteristics of the higher self is inner peace. This is probably the utmost prize and achievement for a human being. When you have inner peace, you have everything.

Lucy from the comic strip *Peanuts* once said that she had inner peace, but she also had "outer obnoxiousness!" I don't think she has quite achieved enlightenment, do you? As we have been learning, the "outer obnoxiousness" reveals whether we have inner peace or not.

Beginning to Learn

My own journey began after I started my first practice. I experienced innumerable failures there that had their origins in my overbearing ego. My education continued with my marriage. My wife had a more powerful ego than I did. When you are up against a superior foe, you have to look at different tactics when doing battle.

Luckily, I was into learning about some of this philosophy after my office experiences. Reading from a number of sources, I had learned about some personal growth issues that made sense to me. One of them was learning to get control over my emotions and my ego.

With my marriage, I knew I was going to lose the war if I continued to fight it out with my wife over our ego issues. Instead, I chose to let my relationship become the structure to try to subdue my ego's control. I use the word *try* purposefully since I have in no way mastered this ego thing. I am working on it, and as time goes on, hopefully I'll get better at it. It's tough to let go.

I think that most of us look at marriage as something that will make our lives complete. It's the romance and love type of stuff that pulls us together. I have to believe that falling in love is nature's way of tricking us into making our commitments to each other.

When we wake up from the sweet narcotic dream of endless love, the real relationship begins. And you know what happens to over half of the marriages these days. When the honeymoon is over, it's time for the egos to start clashing.

A lot of marriages fail because of false expectations about what marriages are supposed to give them. Selfish fantasies of living happily ever after, being rescued from the life you were living, and having your problems taken care of can lead down a destructive, unfulfilled path toward an obvious divorce. Some of these fantasies are downright childish in expectations.

What if we knew ahead of time that marriage was going to be a continual test of how good we are at giving up our egos for the sake of the relationship? The marriage vows should include the promise to place the relationship above the needs of the ego. It would be a great marriage insurance policy if both sides agreed to this promise.

Marriage is a perfect vehicle for us to work on the ego self, even if only one of the partners is doing all the work. Working on relinquishing your ego's total control does not have to be a team sport. I believe this relationship allows us the possibility to see beyond ourselves for the greater good.

Marriage is a powerful testing ground for personal growth and development. We are completely exposed for who we are—with all our faults. It could be said that it is the greatest challenge of our lives, unless you are extremely lucky and marry someone who has his or her ego under control. I've heard where it's better to be a good spouse than to have one. I guess it all depends on what you want out of life.

A Little Help from Ancient Times

Being someone who is more of a student than a teacher of this subject of the higher self, I needed some outside help to bring this subject into the light for further clarification. I hope that what follows helps you as much as it has helped me understand how the mind duality works.

Early Christians recognized the lower and higher self, and they made it a part of their teachings. Aurelius Clemens Prudentius (AD 348–413) was a Christian bishop, theologian, poet, and hymn writer. In the *Psychomachia,* (Battle for the Soul), he described the seven deadly sins and their opposites, the seven contrary virtues.

The sins are illustrative of the works of the ego self, and the virtues are pathways to the higher self. They are direct opposites in all ways. His scheme of vices and virtues works perfectly with the duality description of the mind. Notice the opposing natures of these values in his model.

7 VICES	7 VIRTUES
Pride	Humility
Envy	Kindness
Gluttony	Temperance
Lust	Chastity
Anger	Patience
Greed	Charity
Sloth	Diligence

Prudentius's virtues were specific cures or remedies for the vices he said we needed to overcome in order to have hope for an afterlife. The virtues were to protect against temptations toward the sins.

If you look carefully, all the sins are about the ego self and its obsession with getting. They describe exactly what the ego does and wants. The virtues are descriptive of how the higher self behaves. Knowing about these sins and virtues is absolutely critical for understanding the ego and discovering the higher self. They illustrate the duality of the mind perfectly.

I am reminded of old cartoons where a little angel and a little devil would talk into the ears of one of the characters who was trying to make a decision. The angel would tell the character to do the right thing, and the devil would tell him or her to do the wrong thing. We can hear the ego and higher self—once we have tuned into it—having these conversations all the time if we pay attention to the voices that run through our heads.

Attributes of the Sins

The seven deadly sins are easy to understand but difficult to get rid of. Their ways have become an instinctive part of the lower self, and it's difficult to detect that we are guilty of any one of them. You probably commit some of them every day without believing you are doing anything wrong.

Beware of thinking you are not affected by them since the human capacity for self-delusion is nearly limitless.

In the literary classic, *The Brothers Karamazov*, Dostoevsky writes:

> A man who lies to himself, and believes his own lies, becomes unable to recognize truth, either in himself or anyone else, and he ends up losing respect for himself and others. When he has no respect for anyone, he can no longer love, and in him, he yields to his impulses, indulges in the lowest form of pleasure, and behaves in the end like an animal in satisfying his vices. And it all comes from lying—to others and yourself.

Let's spend a little time getting to know the seven deadly sins and why they are so deadly.

Pride, also known as vanity, is about looking good and believing that being better than others is the way to develop self-esteem. This is self-delusion at its best. Taking pride in ourselves, the way we look, our successes, and our achievements all seem to be good things. But the root of this can be nothing more than a comparison to others. We have to be better than others in some way to feel good about ourselves. We have to defeat others in some way for our pride to work. The ancients believed that pride was the ultimate deadly sin.

Envy is the condition of wanting what someone else has in the way of status, abilities, situations, or traits. Envy makes us believe that if we just had what another had, we would be happy. Envy eats at us, makes us miserable, and keeps our thoughts focused on the lack of whatever we believe we want. Socrates said, "Envy is the ulcer of the soul." Aristotle said, "Envy is pain at the good fortune of others." Human nature appears to be unchanged for a few thousand years.

Gluttony is the desire to consume more than we need or require. It is usually associated with food, but it can be anything that can be consumed or experienced. Wanting more than you really need, wanting something exactly to our specifications without any deviations, and demanding too much from others in the way of time and energy are examples of different types of gluttony. When consumption is pushed to extremes, it becomes almost a form of injustice to others.

Lust is the self-destructive desire for the pleasures of the flesh. It is not only about sexuality; it includes cravings for pleasures of all kinds. Physical and emotional comforts, the best food and wine, the best-looking cars, houses, clothes, and jewelry can all be forms of lust. Lust is a condition where we are enslaved to our senses.

Anger is the sudden releasing of negative, fearful emotions when things don't go the way we want them to. Sometimes the source of our anger comes from when we have held onto pain from past emotional injuries. Something may bring them up again for us to re-experience them. There has to be something that happened or didn't happen in the past that created a feeling of hurt or a void that keeps us from being centered. You also have to feel "right" about whatever made you upset. Being convinced that the other person or event has made you angry, you make them responsible for your anger and believe they have attacked you in some way to justify your retaliation.

Greed is the desire to get more material wealth or gain. By having material success, we can bolster our self-esteem and display how superior we are to others by comparison. Having more things than others—or things that are more expensive than others—allows us to have proof that we are better than others. Personal power is a major motivator for greed. Fear of not having enough for whatever reason is another motivator for being greedy.

And then finally there is *sloth*, which is an avoidance of giving of oneself in many ways. It means not doing what you need to do when you ought to be doing it. By being apathetic about your life, you can't learn, grow, or make any changes in yourself that need changing. A lack of motivation, inactivity, and apathy all seem to go against the ego's desire for getting. But sloth is about wanting something for nothing. Feeling like we are entitled to something and don't want to work for it is a great example of the ego in action.

The seven deadly sins are all about getting, and we learned already that the ego is all about getting. Understanding the seven deadly sins is a great way to know the ego self, but there are many more practical reasons to understand them.

Becoming conscious of the ego self is a way out of a lot of problems we encounter in life. Awareness of any problem is always the first step.

The other side of mind duality—the higher self—represents another choice we have. Just as the seven deadly sins represent the ways of the ego self, the seven contrary virtues represent the ways of the higher self. The virtues are a great way to get to know your higher self. All the virtues extend themselves to others in positive ways.

Attributes of the Virtues

The real paradox of this world is revealed in the duality of the ego and the higher self. The higher self does everything totally opposite from the ego.

Giving is getting. Letting go is having. Not needing anything means being wealthy. Putting oneself last puts you ahead of everyone else. No wonder the higher self is a mystery to most of us. It goes against our common sense.

The higher self is a caretaker of this world and its people—as opposed to all the egos who are just takers. The attributes of the higher self reflect this.

Humility is the absence of the ego self, an absence of false pride, and an absence of overly high ego/self-esteem. There is great power in humility since it takes you out of the unnecessary conflict with other egos. Without conflict, we can concentrate on better things in our lives. C. S. Lewis said, "It doesn't mean that you think less about yourself; it is thinking about yourself less." Humility is necessary for true success in this world; without it, we are unable to learn from the experiences and wisdom of others.

Kindness is an emotional gift we give to others. Lao Tsu said, "Kindness in words gives confidence. Kindness in thinking creates profoundness. Kindness in giving creates love." We can have a positive outlook and a cheerful demeanor that will inspire others to do the same. It is the feeling aspect of quality that we learned is made up of empathy, responsiveness, and ultimately caring.

Temperance comes from having self-control and restraint over our impulses. There is a knowing of when enough is enough and when to be mindful of other's needs. There is a proper balance between your own self-interests and the interests of others. It doesn't have to mean that you don't get what you want. It means that you don't get more than you really need.

Chastity means being chaste physically and mentally. To be pure in thought creates purity in our actions. We become what we think about predominately. Obviously, there is an abstinence insinuation with this one, but it's more in the way of moral wholesomeness.

Patience is a correction to our anger and is the only way to help others deal with their anger without getting involved and escalating the situation. Patience allows things to work out in the manner they are supposed to—as opposed to the way we want them to. We can resolve conflicts peacefully and forgive others with patience. Patience allows us to create a sense of peace, stability, and fellowship.

Charity means being generous, which is the opposite of being greedy. It is giving rather than taking. We can give material goods, time, and energy to help another freely, without any need for reciprocation. Loving others allows us to want to help them. Without a love for humanity, charity is driven by ego. With this virtue, it is sometimes difficult to discern the source of a person's charity.

Diligence allows us to accomplish anything we set out to do if we are persistent and energetic enough. It is an attitude of positive energy that allows us to experience zeal and joy in doing. Never giving up comes from an attitude of positive thinking, which will always be more creative than laziness from a negative attitude.

The seven deadly sins and the seven contrary virtues are some of the most powerful dualities available to describe our split minds. Without them, it would be more than difficult to compare and contrast the ego self and the higher self.

I am so grateful that this invaluable wisdom has been handed down to us for our enlightenment. It fits in perfectly and helps us understand their differences. From them, we are able to improve our awareness about our choices in life.

Our next poem gives us some insight on this very important subject:

The biggest problems in life can be solved
By letting go of the ego, becoming more resolved
To give of our talents and be part of the solution,
Instead of just taking and adding more confusion.

We all have times that seem to tear at our guts,
When we're angry, depressed, or just going nuts.
Just remember that life isn't always an altercation,
But the ego must first learn the art of subjugation.

Here is where real choice in life will reside,
Do we react to the outward or seek answers inside?
Override our lower brains with higher gray matter
So that instincts don't rule and cause all the clatter.

The paradox of life has been uncovered to reveal
An upside down world that hides what is real.
We strive so hard for things that don't matter,
Let's get off of this treadmill and climb up the ladder.

Lesson 13

The Tao, the Ego, and the Higher Self

We are confronted by the great paradox of human life. It is our conditioning
which develops our consciousness; but in order to make full use of this developed
consciousness, we must start by getting rid of the conditioning which developed it.
—Aldous Huxley, *Knowledge and Understanding*

We have talked about the ancient work called the *Tao Te Ching* and its author, Lao Tzu. It was written 2,500 years ago and has endured as a timeless classic that continues to inspire those searching for higher meaning in life. The *Tao Te Ching* has been translated more than any other literary piece in the world, other than the Bible. Throughout this lesson I will be using a few of the translated verses of J. H. McDonald to illustrate its usefulness to understanding the higher self.

The *Tao* is a short work of eighty-one paradoxical and metaphorical passages that let us see that life is not as it appears. It shows us that the ego's perception keeps us from seeing the true nature of reality. The ego is all about an illusion of self; according to the *Tao*, our real power comes from aligning the self with the laws of the universe.

In 1937, Dr. Lionel Giles, a keeper of the Oriental manuscripts at the British Museum said, "Never, surely, has so much thought been compressed into so small a space. The *Tao Te Ching* may fitly be called a 'white dwarf' of philosophical literature, so weighty is it, so compact, and so suggestive of a mind radiating thought at white heat."

Here is a classic verse from the *Tao* explaining a paradox of the higher self and the ego:

> Evolving Individuals hold to the Tao,
> And regard the world as their pattern.
> They do not display themselves:
> Therefore they are illuminated.
> They do not define themselves:
> Therefore they are distinguished.

> They do not make claims:
> Therefore they are credited.
> They do not boast:
> Therefore they advance.

The first part of each sentence contradicts what the ego would normally do, such as putting yourself out front, boasting, and bragging. But when we do just the opposite, we receive what the ego is searching for. Do you like to be around people who talk about themselves or toot their own horns? No one does really.

The bottom line for the *Tao* is that it is all about losing the ego and developing the higher self. The *Tao* is difficult to understand until you read it in this context. It parallels what the seven deadly sins and seven contrary virtues teach us, only from an Eastern perspective. I am using the Tao as another tool to help illustrate the ego and higher self. There is a duality to the *Tao* and the seven sins and virtues. They lead us to the higher self and relinquishing the ego's control. The difference is that one is Eastern philosophy and theology, and the other is Western. We might not recognize East and West as a duality, but it is one of the most important in the world.

> Oh, East is East and West is West, and never the Twain shall meet.
> Till Earth and Sky stand presently at God's great Judgment Seat;
> But there is neither East nor West, Border, nor Breed, Nor Birth,
> When Two strong men stand face to face, though they come from the ends of the earth!
> —Rudyard Kipling, *The Ballad of East and West*

The two strong men meeting here are Aurelius Clemens Prudentius who wrote the seven deadly sins and Lao Tzu who wrote the *Tao*. Representing their respective ends of the earth, they created works that have helped us solve the mystery of the mind's duality. Different points of view, same vision. They both understood that as human beings, we have the opportunity for enlightenment.

Gaining control over the ego self is the solution to so many of our problems. Only the higher self can solve problems created by the ego. Problems can't be solved at the level at which they are created. The ego is the source of most of our problems, and the higher self holds the solutions.

The *Tao* was written 2,500 years ago, and they were thinking about this mystery of life even back then. After all this time, we still haven't gotten the message. I recommend reading the *Tao Te Ching* at some point to get more of a feel of Lao Tzu's insights into reality.

To try to keep it simple, I will use parts of seven passages of the *Tao* that coincide with the seven deadly sins and seven virtues. I will also give you my interpretation of the passages so you can see the similarities between them. I really like using these two great works because they are timeless. I will not use any New Age jargon that may just be a passing fancy.

It is easier to carry an empty cup
than one that is filled to the brim.

The sharper the knife,
the easier it is to dull.

The more wealth you possess,
the harder it is to protect.

Pride brings its own trouble.
When you have accomplished your goal, simply walk away.

This is the pathway to heaven.

We need to try not to identify with our accomplishments and accumulations. Nothing stays the same in nature, and nothing lasts. What happens to our egos when we lose something we identify with? We become despondent, sad, and depressed. We need to keep growing as individuals, and the false pride of our egos just slows us down. Our self-esteem is usually measured by our possessions and accomplishments. "Pride goeth before the fall." The *Tao* teaches us that once we accomplish what we are doing, we should move on to the next project and leave the past behind. Detach, be free, and be open to the possibilities.

True words do not sound beautiful'
Beautiful sounding words are not true.

Wise men don't need to debate.
Men who need to debate are not wise.

Wise men are not scholars'
and scholars are not wise .

The Master desires no possessions.
Since the things she does are for people,
she has more than she needs.

The more she gives to others,
the more she has for herself.

The Tao of Heaven nourishes by not forcing.
The Tao of the Wise person acts by not competing.

This is the evolved way of living. Notice how opposite it is from how we live our lives now. Being humble, good, kind, generous, and selfless are the ways of the *Tao*. The writing is confusing because it is paradoxical in nature. But our higher self is paradoxical and is also difficult to grasp and master. No wonder the higher self is a mystery.

Which is more important, your honor or your life?
Which is more valuable, your possessions or your person?
Which is more destructive, success or failure?
Because of this, great love extracts a great cost,
And true wealth requires a greater loss.
Knowing when you have had enough avoids dishonor
And knowing when to stop will keep you from danger
And bring you a long, happy life.

There is power in needing less. Needing less, wanting less, consuming less, and hoarding less makes one more. Our emotional attachments all come with a resulting burden and cost. This is another paradox that doesn't make any sense to the ego. By not being burdened by needing things or consumption issues, you are free to evolve and grow. The ego believes that getting more is the way to a happy, satisfying life. The higher self knows that less is more.

Five colors will blind the eye.
Five notes deafen one's ear.
Five flavors will make the palate go stale.
Too much activity deranges the mind.
Too much wealth causes crime.
The Master acts on what she feels and not what she sees,
She shuns the latter and prefers to seek the former.

When our senses are tools for the ego's desires, we strive to get the best of whatever we are wanting. That can be the best food, the best wine, the best clothes, the best car, the best house, the best of anything that we value. Our wanting and desires becomes the focus of a good portion of our lives.

When one controls and limits desires, internal growth can begin. Those who are slaves to their desires cannot be aware of anything else and are limited by this perception. With limited and controlled desires, we can be open to more possibilities. Our lives can be richer and fuller without these things.

The best warriors do not use violence
The best generals do not destroy indiscriminately.
The best tacticians try to avoid confrontation.
The best leaders become servants of the people.
This is called the virtue of non- contending.
This is called the power to manage others.
This is called attaining harmony with the heavens.

Force is used to try to manipulate others and gain control over them. Personally we can use anger and threats, governments with their militaries use war. What are we really accomplishing and are the effects going to be lasting? When we allow events and people to unfold and evolve the way they are supposed to—and we practice patience, humility, and composure—we are in tune with the *Tao*. If you push others in order to control them, you will get pushed back in return. Allow the process to take place without interfering.

There is no greater transgression
than condoning people's selfish desires.

There is no greater disaster
than being discontent
and no greater retribution than for greed.

Whoever knows contentment will be at peace forever.

For most of us, there is never enough. That is a sad thought. It creates a constant feeling of dissatisfaction. That is not a good way to go through life. When one doesn't have a need for something, there is always enough of it to go around. Is life just about striving to get more so that the ego will be satisfied? If the ego is never satisfied, why become a hamster on a running wheel without a destination in order to try to unsuccessfully fulfill its unreasonable needs? It has been said that the richest man is the one who needs the least.

Those who know others are intelligent;
Those who know themselves are truly wise.
Those who master others are strong;
Those who master themselves have true power.

Those who know they have enough are wealthy.
Those who persist will reach their goal.
Those who keep their course have a strong will.
Those who embrace death will not perish,
But have life everlasting.

To know, master, persevere, maintain, and endure requires energy devoted to the right things. When you drop your desires for personal power and gain, you will have true power and gain given to you. Getting control over the ego-self is a lifelong process. And when it's over, we will leave the world a better place.

The Results of the Higher Self

The results of the higher self can be described as opposite of the results of the ego. Instead of all the bad and negative feelings that are a result of the ego, try to imagine feeling the opposite.

The higher self offers everything we are searching for in this world: happiness, peace, joy, inspiration, satisfaction, and love. It is what we are all seeking in our lives. We are just going about it in the wrong way. We all want the same things in life; we are just using the wrong path to get there.

The ego-self cannot get us what we truly desire. It actually gives us the opposite. What seems right for us is wrong. This paradox makes our world so mysterious.

The seven deadly sins and the *Tao Te Ching* have hopefully brought some clarity to this mystery of life. The mystery has been uncovered and revealed. Where do we go from here?

Our summary poem is about how the authors of long ago had this figured out. Why has it taken us so long to learn what they taught us?

Ancient masters figured out the mysteries of life,
Our inside-out world filled with conflict and strife
This absurdity so confusing long ago was revealed,
Along with its answers remarkably concealed.

It's much more blessed to give than to receive.
Why is that so hard for us to conceive?
The ego keeps trying to get what it desires,
Getting more than others is what it requires.

That's a dead-end street that they understood well,
Would lead us to conflict and create our own hell.
Lessons from these wise men you would think we'd extol,
But our ego-brain is stubborn and steadfastly in control.

Mankind's higher self on the whole is well hidden,
As our egos waste time grabbing fruit most forbidden.
Our destinies lie in accepting this simple fact,
The train we're riding is on the wrong track.

Lesson 14

Choices

Good choices come from experience, and experience comes from having made bad choices.
—Anonymous

The subject of how we make our choices in life is most intriguing and receives less attention than it deserves. Making good choices is paramount to creating a happy, rewarding life. The converse of that statement is equally true.

How do we learn to make good choices? How do we teach others to make good choices? Is it even possible? It has been said many times and in many ways that we are the sum total of all our choices. When we look back and reflect on our lives, it is easy to see what we did right and what we did wrong with our choices. Hindsight is twenty-twenty!

We can learn from our mistakes though, and if we become a bit philosophical, we might be able to acknowledge that our mistakes were possibly more important to our growing process than the right choices we have made.

Maybe we have to make our mistakes. Is it possible to really learn something about life without experiencing it firsthand? I think not. I have to believe that is one of the reasons human nature hasn't changed for all of recorded history. It seems that we all have to learn the hard way in order to really understand the significance and value of our lessons.

Maybe our choices reflect our present level of ego control, knowledge, awareness, state of mind, wisdom, education, maturity, inherent temperament, values, perceptions, and the influence of family, friends, and culture. In other words, our choices reflect who you are at this moment—and your choices come from all that you are. Is this really a choice?

You can't easily change who you are. Just ask any psychiatrist, psychologist, therapist, or counselor how difficult it is. If you make your choices based upon who you are, it stands to reason that you can't easily change your choices without changing who you are. Does this make any sense? When you make a choice, you are revealing who you are at that moment. Your present choices are creating, defining, and narrowing your life's path.

Baylor University neuroscientist Dr. Read Montague (a fellow at Princeton's Institute for Advanced Study) wrote a book about how we make choices. *Why Choose This Book? How We Make Decisions* uses the latest research in psychology and neuroscience. He says that human choices are brain computations that involve valuations, choosing between one value and another. We've gone over value systems and how they work. Values run us like computer programs.

Do We Really Have a Choice?

If some of our value-based choices are predetermined by our genetically created temperament, is this really a choice?

Let's explore some of the basics of our choices and decisions. It seems that we have to deal with the duality issue with our mistakes, which states that we can't recognize one side of anything without comparing it to the other.

The duality nature of our lives allows us to experience one aspect that can be interpreted as unpleasant (bad) in order to truly appreciate the opposite side that we experience as pleasant (good).

It is in our nature to try to avoid unpleasant experiences, but I don't think that avoidance works as a viable option. It seems that we have to experience a certain amount of negativity and sorrow in order to truly experience contentment and joy. In other words, we have to make our mistakes and suffer our consequences. If we don't make the mistakes, there isn't a lesson to learn. If we learn our lessons or learn new information, we can make different choices.

Our true levels of awareness or consciousness don't grow easily from non-experiential information. It requires us to actually participate in something to be able to feel it fully and be able to understand the ramifications of our actions or inactions. That is why we have to make mistakes. It is a pathway to higher consciousness if we choose to accept our lessons as they happen to us. When we make mistakes and learn from them, awareness is heightened.

We may believe that we are in control of our choices. Are we really? You have seen how some of our choices are already made for us with the duality component of our temperaments. Many of our preferences are genetically predetermined. How often are we really choosing or do we just let our ingrained likes and dislikes predetermine the choices for us?

We make choices all the time: Cheerios or Corn Flakes, this TV program or a movie, chocolate or vanilla, this one or that one. These kinds of choices really don't matter in the grand scheme of things. But how do we form these preferences? Why do we like one thing over another? *Because we just do!* I say that most of our decisions in life are made this way.

If you have children, you know they are born with certain likes and dislikes without ever having been learned choices. Our predetermined and ingrained preferences become our steering currents as we float along in our life vessels. So where is there real choice in this life?

I believe that our true choices are when we choose between the ego and the higher self. I believe that the most meaningful lessons in our lives are designed for us to let go of the ego's control. (Please think about this statement for a while because it's really important.) The ego is in denial of real choice and wants to keep us in a box so we don't change or grow.

As long as the ego is in charge of our lives, there really isn't much choice. You want what you want, when you want it. As long as the ego is in charge of our lives, we are just experiencing the results of our egos in action. We don't have too much control over what happens to us, and with the ego in charge, we don't have too much control over how we handle what happens to us.

The only true choices we make are when we override what the ego wants and do what the higher self says to do. It's as simple as that. There, in a nutshell, is the most important and biggest challenge of our lives. I hope you can grasp the significance of this profound concept.

Sometimes we have internal conflict about certain decisions. We know we should do something, but we rationalize an alternative. We know we shouldn't make that choice, but we do it anyway. A simple example would be having that dessert when we are on a diet. We just couldn't help ourselves, could we! Which part of the self couldn't help itself?

Our Multi-Level Brains

Understanding the multilevel brain system offers some help in why we have conflicting internal conversations. Recognizing that our lower brains have different conversations than our higher brains is probably as good an explanation as any. Which one is in charge? What can be the best choice for one of our brains might not be the most comfortable choice for the others. There can be a lot of indecision because of the internal differences of opinion inside our brains.

One of the problems with choice for human beings is that we are multileveled beings. Being human is a difficult task for us all with our dualities, our different levels of awareness, our different brains, and their functions. It's all very confusing and challenging. Plus we have the ultimate mystery of wondering about the purpose of all this. It's a wonder we aren't all crazy!

It is widely accepted that we have three completely different brains that act like three interconnected computers. Even though they are connected, each brain has its own special type of intelligence and value system. Each can operate independently to an extent.

Neurologist Paul MacLean, MD, in his groundbreaking book, *The Triune Brain in Evolution*, said that these brains have special intelligence, subjectivity, sense of time and space, and memory. He said, "The three brains are connected to each other, but each seems to operate as an independent brain system with its own distinct capacities." He appropriately labeled all this the triune brain. Dr. MacLean said, "We are obligated to look at ourselves and the world through the eyes of three quite different mentalities."

The functionality of our trilogy of brains is similar to the concept of humans having bodies, minds, and spirits. Also it reflects the trilogies found in many religions and philosophies.

One part of the brain (the brain stem and cerebellum) is called the reptilian brain because it functions in the same way as a reptile's brain. It evolved hundreds of millions of years ago and controls the bodies breathing, heart rates, temperature, and other functions automatically without any conscious control. It also functions with basic fundamental needs, such as survival instincts, sex drive, hunger, thirst, and just about anything that is instinctual. It plays an important role in aggressive behavior, territoriality, and violence, and it functions without any true thinking or rationalization.

The basic ruling emotions of anger, sadness, disgust, fear, surprise, and happiness originate from this brain. When rage takes over, this brain takes over our actions. When we say we couldn't help ourselves when we made some impulsive action, we are really saying that our reptilian brain made us do it. Getting control of our impulsive behaviors means getting rational control over this brain. And it is accomplished by accessing our other, more evolved brains.

The next brain is called the old mammalian brain because early, lower-evolved mammals also had this type of brain. All mammals have certain capabilities that are similar to ours. This brain is where memory is stored and is coupled with emotional qualities that help to create our feelings. Retained memories of fear are located here and influence our interpretations of present moments.

Emotion, behavior, attention, motivation, and learning come from this complex set of brain structures, which are also called the *limbic system*. We react to certain events in certain ways with our emotions and feelings that can be interpreted with the higher brain. Parts of the limbic brain include the hypothalamus, the thalamus, the hippocampus, the pituitary gland, and the amygdala.

The outer level of the brain, which is called the neocortex, is responsible for higher cognitive functions, which distinguishes humans from lower animals. Dr. MacLean referred to the cortex as "the mother of invention and father of abstract thought."

The neocortex is divided into the right and left hemispheres as we previously discussed. In each of these hemispheres, different lobes have different functions. These are important in higher-order thinking skills, such as music, math, spatial conceptualization, intuition, and imagination.

The people who study these things believe there is no center of consciousness in our brains. The different brains that come in and out of control create moment-to-moment consciousness. Whichever one is in charge at the moment defines your reality and your actions.

MacLean was first to show that the higher brain does not dominate the others; the lower brains dominate it. He says, "Our emotions usually override our higher mental functions if it is aroused by an appropriate stimulus." New brain-imaging studies have proven this to be true beyond a shadow of a doubt. The brain's wiring relies on emotion over intellect in our decisions.

In fact, people who lack emotions because of brain injuries often have difficulty making decisions at all. The brain stores emotional memories of past decisions that drive people's choices. Antonio Damasio said, "What makes us rational is not to suppress our emotions, but tempering them in a positive way."

When we allow the external world to control our behaviors, we are allowing our lower brains (reptilian and old mammalian) to take over. Our emotions are a reaction to outside stimuli without any choices by us. We don't choose our emotional reactions. Stepping back and becoming self-aware can profoundly alter the way our brains work. It can activate the neocortex regions, which gives us some control over our emotions.

More Help from Dr. Glasser

Part of the solution to this problem comes from Dr. William Glasser with his choice theory, which states that we don't have to be controlled by external events. We don't have to go through life just reacting to what happens to us.

He states that there are four components of human behavior: doing, thinking, feeling, and physiology (heart rate, sweating, breathing, headaches, etc.).

Dr. Glasser believes that people need to see that they *do* have choices. Most people are more in tune with their feelings than anything else, and they let their feelings run their behaviors. (This is where there is no choice.) This way, what happens to us determines how we react and then behave. This is very destructive to relationships.

You don't have any control over your feelings and your physiology, but you do have some control over your thinking. You have the most control over your doing. By recognizing that these components are all a part of us, we don't have to be slaves to our feelings and physiology—and we can be in more control of our lives. We are free to choose our responses to outside events.

Dr. Glasser explains that we can allow the higher brain to override the lower brain when we make decisions. We don't have to succumb to physical discomfort when choosing. We can use the rational brain to make decisions. He says that when we allow outside events to control us, they will destroy our ability to create satisfying relationships, which creates disconnectedness. This is a source of human problems, such as mental illness, drug addiction, violence, crime, and spousal abuse.

He also describes something similar to the seven deadly sins and seven virtues that he uses in his choice theory treatments, which he calls the seven deadly habits and seven caring habits. He says that most of us miss out on a very important requisite that can satisfy our needs for closeness and connectedness in our relationships. Our overuse of the seven deadly habits creates destructive relationships.

His "habits" will help us understand how we might want to change our behaviors in order to create happier, more satisfying relationships. Our task is to stop negative habits and replace them with behaviors that are more positive. Let's let the higher brain start taking over.

7 DEADLY HABITS	7 CARING HABITS
Criticizing	Supporting
Blaming	Encouraging
Complaining	Listening
Nagging	Accepting
Threatening	Trusting
Punishing	Respecting
Bribing, rewarding to control	Negotiating differences

With the information you have received so far, you can easily see that the seven deadly habits are nothing more than our egos at work, and the seven caring habits are our higher selves in action. Make a list of your deadly habits and check to make sure that you aren't guilty of too many of them. The people around you will all thank you. Your ability to choose has hopefully been made a little clearer.

Thanks for all your help, Dr. Glasser!

I still believe that the ability to choose properly comes from who we are at the present moment. Giving this advice to many people would fall on deaf ears. The people who would be helped most by Dr. Glasser's work would be those who have made enough mistakes to understand the need to make changes. They are sick and tired of getting negative results. I agree with his theories wholeheartedly, but we need to be willing and able to listen before we can hear his message.

Ego Equals Fear and Anxiety/Higher Self Equals Trust and Peace

A difficult lesson is learning that we are not in control of every aspect of our lives. And that is very unnerving for a lot of us to accept. Giving up control requires letting go and allowing life to unfold as it is going to.

Many years ago, I was listening to a lecture by a highly respected dentist who was informative and wise. He had a lot of great information about his subject matter, but he also interjected bits of personal philosophy that I found most enlightening.

He had recently lost his daughter in an automobile accident. It was every parent's nightmare. I could imagine nothing worse than losing a child. I asked him during a break how he managed to get through that tragic event. He thought for a while and then quietly said, "You just have to trust the process."

I had to think about that for a long, long time before it registered. *You just have to trust the process.* I held that idea in my head and couldn't shake it. My daughter was about to have her first birthday. I couldn't love anything anymore than her. If I lost her, could I trust the process? I couldn't answer that one in the way I would have wanted because I knew I couldn't. His ability to handle his loss spoke volumes about the person he was.

We all know people who have gone through horrible, life-altering events. We are all fearful of something like this happening to our loved ones. Trusting the process is a choice that allows us to let go of the things in life we can't—or really shouldn't—control. Trusting the process is a leap of faith in letting go of fear and the ego's control. Trusting the process is a prime characteristic of the higher self.

It's not easy to trust the process, but it is simple. With trust comes an inner peace that can't be explained to the ego. The ego brings fear and anxiety. With the higher self, we experience the opposite; trust and peace are our rewards. Accessing the higher self is the key to all this, but there are important concepts that allow us to grow in this direction. Let's explore some of these as we read our next lesson.

Our next summary poem explores choice and some feelings one might have as we try to understand our options:

So many choices, so many paths you can go.
Just do what feels right, there's no other way to know.
How else will you find what makes you happy or sad?
That this one is good and this one is bad.

Life is contrived when you think in this style.
Our feelings control us if you ponder this for a while.
It's not our fault when we act just like fools.
Our instincts keep telling us what are the rules.

We are cruising on autopilot, living a dream,
But this isn't free will, as it may seem.
What appears to be choice, there's no real need to decide.
Our preprogrammed brain is where our preferences preside.

Our only real choice creates the life we will be living.
It's all about the taking, or it's all about the giving.
A human becoming instead of a human being,
You're in control of the vision you'll be seeing.

Lesson 15

Accessing the Higher Self

Every man is a divinity in disguise, a god playing the fool.
—Ralph Waldo Emerson, *The Conduct of Life*

Actions and behaviors sourced by the higher self will give you better results than those sourced by the ego. The problem is that most of us are stuck in ego mode and can't get out of it. How to access the higher self is the million-dollar question.

I think that the higher self is analogous to any other aspect of the mind or body. You have to use it—or you are going to lose it. An example would be when you have a broken bone in your arm, and your doctor places the limb in a cast for a prolonged time. Your affected muscles atrophy from disuse. It takes a long time after the cast is off and a lot of exercise to build up those muscles again.

Because of the values of our ego-based, materialistic culture, we have lost the use of the higher self and have hidden it away. We need to get it out, dust it off, begin to exercise it, and nourish it back to health.

The first step is to recognize that we have lost sight of the higher self and what we really want out of our lives. We can start using its power and start getting the results we have been unsuccessfully trying to get with our egos. Awareness of the situation is crucial.

There has to be an intention made at this point. You have to make the commitment to start letting go of the ego's control and allow the higher self to enter your consciousness. This intention is the greatest of all you can make. Without a conscious intention, you will revert to what is instinctual and natural as you react to the outside world through your ego's perceptions. This is where true choice lives.

Once you have made this intention, your choices will begin to fall in line. Don't be too hard on yourself when you begin; it is a lifelong journey. Lao Tzu said, "A journey of a thousand miles begins with a single step."

What is Your Purpose?

Here are some great questions to ask yourself as you are developing your intentions. What is the purpose of your life? What are you really doing with your life? Could there be more to your life than what you are presently doing with it?

If you are looking for more—or want more out of life—developing a purpose with a higher intention may be the answer for you. What does that even mean? Before we can truly appreciate the answer, we must understand the different purposes available to us. Our categories of purposes happen to coincide with our multilevel brains. Each brain views the world from a different perspective, and each has a totally different purpose to fill.

The reptilian brain is all about survival. Keeping alive, safe, and nourished are its functions and purposes. Our first purpose choice is all about physical needs. Luckily, in our present-day world, most of us have these needs met without too much difficulty. For those who are homeless and destitute, this becomes their day-to-day purpose. But our survival needs can be more than just physical needs once the next level brain makes an alliance with the reptilian brain. The ego's needs may become just as important as the physical, and they can feel just as real.

The mammalian brain is the source of our emotions. Here is where the bulk of our temperament and ego are sourced. Being who you are—by your nature and searching out your desires and preferences—becomes a life-long journey for most of us. Just going through life, liking this and not liking that, wanting this and avoiding that, is an unconscious purpose. Working to exercise our genetic preferences is the purpose most of us now have. Its purpose is to be able to get what it wants and do as it pleases. The ego-self and its desires are the most important at this level.

The higher-level brain is the home of all rational thought, creativity, and higher-level thinking. We can make the ultimate choice: to live by the higher self. I have to believe the higher self sources the higher purpose. I also have to believe the soul is linked to the higher self. Then it's possible that validation of your soul can become your purpose in life.

Finding your soul's purpose is one of the most important things you can do in this world. We all have special gifts to give to the world, which is what I call the soul's purpose. But we can't give when we live our lives only trying to get what the ego wants.

The ego has a number of tricks up its sleeve that help keep us from reaching out to the higher self. It will stop at nothing in order to remain in control.

A Victim Mentality

When the ego has been exposed, invalidated, restrained, or defeated, it is a normal response to have hurt feelings. The severity of this ego pain can do tremendous damage to the ego's self-esteem and self-image, especially while growing up.

People can be so affected by these hurts that it actually becomes a major influence in their behaviors and attitudes. We all have seen this in action with our own hurts or those around us. We can become victims to whoever was responsible for this pain.

Playing the victim and really believing the self is a victim robs us of so many opportunities in life. Blaming another for one's inadequacies keeps us from being fully present in the now. We become a prisoner to the past as it influences what we do in the present and limits our future possibilities.

In his book, *Unapologetically You: Reflections on Life and the Human Experience*, behavioral scientist Dr. Steve Maraboli states, "The victim mindset dilutes the human potential. By not accepting responsibility for our circumstances, we greatly reduce our power to change them.

One of the most significant choices we can make as human beings is learning how to let go of past hurts we can't seem to forget and forgiving those who caused the pain. This is an area where real choice lives. When you choose forgiveness, it is a choice sourced by the higher self. Forgiveness opens up a wondrous process that leads us past our egos.

This process will allow us to miraculously let go of resentment, sadness, hurt, or anger. Even though this event happened in the past, we can relive it when something or someone triggers an exaggerated response in us. Negative feelings can be brought forward and can influence how we react or respond to situations. These negative emotions can't help but create a negative outlook on life.

Someone in the past did something to us that hurt us badly enough that we can't let go of it. We believe we were victimized and violated. In our heart of hearts, we know it was his or her fault—and we can't or won't let go of what he or she did to us.

As long as we hold on to those hurts, we can't fully benefit from all the information that we have learned so far. These hurts block us from growing and letting go of our egos because they are sourced from our egos.

Being a victim reveals just how deeply controlled by your ego you really are. Those who have a victim mentality are demonstrating that they have an ego-driven mentality. This may be a confusing aspect of understanding how the ego works.

One of the fundamental characteristics of the ego is its need for getting. Where is the payoff for being a victim? Before we expose the payoff, let's look at how the victim mentality works.

Here is a list of what a victim might think or feel or do:

- feels sorry for self
- plays the martyr
- uses past abuse as an excuse not to try
- makes excuses for behavior
- refuses to acknowledge own power
- blind to personal power
- sees the world as a place of lack

- whiner or Debbie Downer
- overly anxious or afraid
- negative mind-set
- acts helpless and powerless
- feel like people are out to get you
- have a chip on your shoulder
- blames others for mistakes

Society seems to have somehow embraced a victim mentality in recent times. Especially from our politicians who have learned that victimized constituents are easily manipulated when promised that their needs will be taken care of—if they just vote for them. It isn't healthy for anyone to not be responsible for themselves. Being a victim keeps us from creating, accomplishing, learning, growing, giving, etc. In other words, one chooses to pass on all the things in life that will ultimately give us joy and happiness.

One of the payoffs from this is that being a victim gives them the right to be stuck. That way, they are exactly where the ego wants them to be, and they won't escape its clutches. They have been hurt by someone and can't accept responsibility because of how they feel.

People who are victimized want sympathy and expect the help of others to do things for them. Inaction, laziness, sloth, or whatever you want to call it is the result. They refuse to overcome this experience. They want pity and lots of it. This is the big payoff. The ego always wants—and always needs—more.

One thing in this world is certain: you get out of life what you put into it. A victim mentality is a self-fulfilling prophecy; your life has a way of becoming what your dominant thoughts and emotions are. If you think victim thoughts all day long, you will be sure to experience life as a victim and no one outside you will solve your problems. It is a real shame that people can't see how being a victim negatively affects them.

A victim mentality will create a life with few possibilities. The way out is to let go of these past hurts and take responsibility for your present and future. Forgiveness is the way.

I Can't Do It

A victim mentality also translates to an "I can't do it" mentality. I can't do this, and I can't do that because of this excuse. They are victims. They can't solve their problems, be happy, or be successful. They can't get jobs, lose weight, or stop drinking or smoking or whatever else is their problem.

A victim mentality is probably one of the biggest obstacles that keeps people stuck and makes them incapable of true happiness. It just so happens that the foundational lessons of the T-Code were created to help you with this one.

There is good news. Some of those hurts you carry *can* be let go—and you can stop being a victim. If we understood people and ourselves more, maybe we wouldn't take some people's mistakes so personally. Maybe we could look at the hurtful situation from a different perspective and create a new interpretation of it that makes us see it in a new light.

Any situation where temperaments clash due to opposite and competing values can end in a bad way. Feelings can be hurt when one side or the other inadequately handles emotional situations. The opportunities for conflict are virtually endless, but we have the knowledge to begin the process of letting go of the hurts by understanding the T-Code. We have the knowledge to start forgiving others for just being who they are.

Forgiveness is the Key.

Forgiveness is the starting point that also happens to be one of the universal commonalities of most major religions. It most assuredly is a key to unleashing the higher self. It begins with forgiving ourselves. It begins with allowing ourselves to not be the center of the universe. It begins with allowing ourselves to be capable of being wrong. It begins with seeing ourselves as we really are: imperfect, incomplete, and not all-knowing. This is the opposite of what the ego tries to tell us. Forgiveness opens the door to the higher self by closing the door on the ego's domination over life's perceptions.

Forgiveness seems to be the foremost lesson we have to learn in order to embrace the higher self. It's also one of the most difficult. So much has to be in place for us to be able to forgive. Forgiveness is not just letting people off the hook for what we think they have done to us. We have to change our interpretations of and perspectives on what they did to us.

The T-Code has given us much valuable information about why people are who they are. It also allows us to see that everyone has deficiencies in their temperaments. No one is perfect. We are all guilty of not understanding one another and taking what others do to us in personal ways.

The ego, which is really the false self, has to be seen for what it is and what it does. If we can overlook what others do because they are under the spell of their egos and are temporarily insane (that's how I justify their mistakes), we open up the possibilities for forgiveness.

Forgiveness can only occur when you begin to recognize that all people make mistakes. We shouldn't take their limitations personally. Life is nothing more than a grand dance between imperfect beings: one imperfect person not knowing what his or her actions will cause and another imperfect being who has innate fragility. If we didn't have the capacity to be hurt, the other person's actions would have no effect.

When someone wrongs us and our feelings get hurt, it can be a way of exposing our weaknesses so we can work on becoming stronger. We can also go on the offensive and get revenge by hurting them more than they hurt us. Which way do you think is best?

Forgiveness is the greatest and most important lesson we have to learn as human beings. Jesus said, "Forgive us our trespasses as we forgive those who trespass against us." He said this because it is so crucial to be able to live our lives fully.

In order to have forgiveness for all the mistakes we have made, we have to be able to forgive others who have made mistakes that have affected us. The rules have to apply to everyone. With forgiveness, the way we think about the self, others, and the world can be changed.

With forgiveness, all the wrongs of the past can be let go, which will release the hurt feelings and the negative thoughts that really eat at people. It never ceases to amaze me how we can hang on to childhood issues as adults. The stuff we carry with us affects our relationships, and sometimes we commit the same errors to our loved ones. It is crazy how this works. We are all victims of victims. Our egos are victims of other egos who have been victimized.

It has been reported that these sorts of deep-seated negative emotions of the ego will cause our bodies to become susceptible to diseases like cancer and heart conditions. It seems to me that as long as we are driven by the ego, we all need therapy of some sort!

The Ego is Insane.

The ego is really the definition of insanity. Think about it. It wants to believe it is the center of the universe. This is the foundation from which everything else is driven. It's all a house of cards from there. The insecure foundation tries to build false support by getting and accumulating things. A description of insanity is doing the same things over and over and expecting different results. The ego keeps using the same old worn-out playbook and expects to get a different outcome.

One of the distinguishing characteristics of the ego is that everything it does is based upon fear. You might not believe this statement, but it is fundamental for understanding and letting go of the ego's control. The ego self is really a scaredy-cat—and for very good reasons!

The ego has to get things in order to try to bolster its self-esteem because it knows it is flawed. The ego tries to hide behind the false image it presents to others. It is afraid that it will be exposed as a fraud and a fake.

What happens when someone exposes another's flaws with criticism, sarcasm, gossip, rumors, or invalidation? The ego feels attacked. Its very existence is threatened. Intense feelings of anger, rage, humiliation, embarrassment, and sadness can occur. These feelings are sometimes so intense that they can't be forgotten or forgiven when the ego has been wounded. It's the other person's fault that it feels so horrible. The ego must retaliate for survival or withdraw in shame. It has been exposed for what every human being truly is: flawed, incomplete, and capable of errors. If not for the person exposing it, it could continue to be the center of the universe.

The hurt lasts and lasts and enters the subconscious. It comes up when a similar event occurs or when it seems like it might occur. The ability to respond to a situation is influenced by this never-ending hurt. We are blocked from living in the present. We relive our hurts over and over. It's time we wake up and see the ego for what it really is.

The choice of forgiveness is a mandatory step. Don't look any further for the answer to what you should do. Start letting go of any needless hurt and judgment you are carrying around. Until the choice of forgiveness is made, you will be reacting from your interpretation of past external events, which will keep you from living in the present moment.

There are no possibilities for acting differently from how you have always acted. You are being controlled by the past, and you are not in charge of the present moment. There is no choice when you are in this state of being. Without forgiveness, history has a way of repeating itself. Without forgiveness, you will not be given another chance to change your reality.

The lack of forgiveness is a sure indicator that you are stuck in a lower-brain mentality since your emotions and fears are located there. Your higher self can't be accessed because your ego self and the primitive brain are in charge.

If you want to rise above the chaos, conflict, and hurt of this world, you will find that forgiveness will have to be included in your process. Let go of the ego's control. Begin to use the lessons of the T-Code to help forgive others and yourself. It will do you and the world wonders.

We Are All Connected.

There is scientific evidence that each of us can do wonders by just being who we are—either in a positive or negative way. While we hold on to resentments and pain from past hurts, we unconsciously project them to those around us. Our interactions and relationships with others are deeply affected by what we hold inside with our thoughts and feelings.

We are all connected to others in the world with the neurochemical reactions in our brains and the magnetic and electrical fields generated by our hearts. Our hearts and brains are connected based upon the thoughts and emotions we produce.

Every thought and corresponding feeling we have sends out an electromagnetic wave from the base of our heart, according to Rollin McCraty, PhD, the leading researcher of the Institute of HeartMath. The core of HeartMath's philosophy is that the heart physically and metaphorically is the key to tapping into intelligence that can provide us with fulfillment.

The heart produces the largest rhythmic electromagnetic field in the body, and this field is influenced by our emotions (positive and negative). Spectromagnetic analysis of the magnetic field shows that our emotional information is encoded in it. Through the heart's pulses, it sends energy in the form of a blood pressure wave. Researchers have seen that changes in the electrical activity of brain cells occur in relation to the changes in the blood pressure wave.

The world is made up of electrical and magnetic fields, which our present-day understanding of the atom reveals. Our hearts and minds can influence both of these fields. These fields affect our lives—and the lives of those around us. What you do affects those around you in a positive or negative manner, whether you are aware of it or not. It is postulated that our realities are actually created by a combination of our thinking and our emotions. Our realities can be created by the ego or the higher self. We can make the choice.

It is the marriage of our thoughts (electrical) and our emotions (magnetic) that creates our electromagnetic aura both positive and negative. Gaining control over our thoughts and emotions by our higher self is where mastery of this life resides. It is as simple and profound as that. Of course it is not easy to do but this entire book has been preparing you for this. Now you know what you need to do to recreate your life– if you choose.

How great would it be if we could create a chain reaction with self-awareness that positively influenced others to do the same? This might make us see how we can make a difference in the world. It's easy to say that what we do as individuals has no effect upon what others do. We might be surprised to know what the combination of our minds and hearts are capable of creating in the world. We need to understand that we can influence others in good and bad ways.

As long as you continue to allow the external events of the world to control you by only reacting to what happens to you, you will be a part of the world's problems. Once you allow the higher self to become the source in your actions, you will become part of the solution. People around you will respond to your new and improved way of being.

Your ego has conflict built into its reactions by instinct. Your higher self has the means for conflict resolutions that are only accessible by choice. Ultimate freedom is deciding how anybody or anything outside ourselves will affect us (an ego reaction or a higher self-response).

The Distinction is Clear.

The distinction is very clear for us. We can create an earthly experience from two completely opposite sources: the ego, which is sourced by fear, or the higher self. As long we see ourselves as separate and independent centers of the universe—mostly concerned with getting what the ego wants—we will reap the harvest the ego sows. There is no escaping this fact.

You can try all you want to become the best ego-centered individual you can become, but it will never lead you to a life where happiness and contentment reside.

Problems that arise from an ego-based consciousness can never be solved because there is no real solution at this level. That is our plight on earth in a nutshell. Unless you recognize that your ego is the source of most of your problems, then there is no way out. Those are pretty strong words, but I stand by them.

As long as the ego is in charge, we are going to travel down a predetermined path. With our inherent genetic temperament and preprogrammed preferences, we are bound to have certain problems and conflicts along the way. Our instinctual behaviors from our lower brains will cause us to react to situations in ways that will get predictably negative results. This is pretty much a lengthy, expanded definition of fate.

Wikipedia says that fate is a predetermined course of events. It may be conceived as a predetermined future, whether in general or of an individual. It is a concept based on the belief that there is a fixed natural order to the cosmos.

The higher self has a different path that I call destiny. Destiny is like fate, but a person's actions can influence it. The higher self and its higher purpose can have incredible potential for greatness. This potential can be found within each of us.

We all have the power to change our lives and the lives of those around us in a positive way with our higher self's thinking and emotions. There may come a time where humankind experiences its ultimate negative fate from the conflict of egos, whatever that may be. The evolution of humankind will depend upon the potential power of greatness and its expression to arise from the ashes. I believe this is our destiny.

Getting to a place where we can access the higher self and fulfill our destinies requires letting go of the ego's control. Hopefully, this lesson will begin the process. Forgiveness is a major part of the process.

Our summary poem is all about forgiveness. It is so important to all of us, all over the world.

I forgive you.
With these three simple words, the heavens swirled.

I release you.
And everything is now right with the world.

I'm letting go.
Freeing all of my pain and stress,

I've finally forgotten.
How could I have been such a mess?

You'll never know.
There was much hate I was holding within.

I never knew
That healing this wound was for me to begin.

You, my scorn,
For so long, it seemed quite prudent.

Who'd have believed
You were the teacher and I, the student?

I feel so relieved.
Why did the hurt have to last that long?

I love you now,
For helping me to become this strong.

Lesson 16

Where Do We Go Now?

We love our habits more than our income, often more than our life.
—Bertrand Russell, *Sceptical Essays*

I would like to start this lesson by saying that I do not have any expectations that everyone will be suddenly transformed or permanently impacted by the information in this book. As much as I would like to make a difference in this world, I know how difficult it is to change people's perceptions about anything. There have been times when I wondered whether it was worth the effort to write a book like this if it might not have any appreciable impact on anyone. It was obviously just a sloth (one of the seven deadly sins) moment.

Real learning is a process, and awareness is the first step. This book will be a great starting point for some. For others, this book might be the right information at the right time to make some lasting changes for the better. And of course, some won't be interested at all in this material.

Some will, some won't, some do, and some don't. Everyone is at different places in the world. It is impossible for us to judge what path is right for others. Who knows the lessons each of us needs to learn, the way we need to learn them, and the proper timing for us to learn? Absolutely no one!

How often have we been introduced to potentially life-changing information, but we didn't use it because it was easier and more comfortable to keep doing things the way we were used to? The end result of reading this book can be no different than many other self-help books that resulted in no measurable personal change in behaviors. There are reasons why this happens. The adage that you can't teach an old dog new tricks speaks volumes. It's just part of human nature.

Before we go any further, I would like to clarify something about our humanness that is characteristically paradoxical by its nature. It is quite human to not learn lessons and stay stuck in our egos. But it is also in our nature to learn, grow, and evolve. We just haven't made this concept mainstream at this point in time. Maybe we just don't know any better at this point in time. This paradox is all part of the mystery and wonder of being human.

155

In rare instances, some of us "old dogs" are able to learn "new tricks." I will show you how real change is possible in your life and how it can happen. But don't get your hopes up too high because it's not easy even with the proper clarification.

Let's investigate why it is so difficult for human beings to make changes when they know they should or could do something for the better. I believe it is one of the most important ramifications of the mysteries of human nature. Why do we not sometimes learn our lessons and make improvements to ourselves when we know we should? Why do we hold on to our ways so vigorously? What is wrong with us?

The Ego Will Not Tolerate Changes in Self-identification.

As we have already explored in detail, the ego is the self-proclaimed center of its universe. It is right and justifiable in everything it does. Its perception is keenly accurate in its mind, and everyone else's ways have to be flawed if they don't match up.

The ego can't be invalidated in any way—or it couldn't possibly keep up the charade it puts on. It identifies with some of the silliest things and is not open to changing them once they have been placed in its collection. The ego in its most basic state is fearful. All ego-based emotions are based upon fear. Change invalidates it and scares it to death! Change is sometimes scarier than death itself.

Even some of the most destructive habits can become a major part of its identification. Excessive smoking, drinking, gambling, eating, drugs, and sex can become so entrenched in the ego that it is virtually impossible to stop without letting go of control.

This is why rehabilitation for these destructive habits can be so difficult. One thing that needs to take place before they can be overcome is an emotional ego deprogramming. The ego has survival reactions that are as strong as our instincts for avoiding life-threatening events. Getting rid of addictions can sometimes mean giving up the ego's control. That is very difficult for most of us—and impossible for some.

Have you ever known someone who was diagnosed with a life-threatening illness that was caused by bad habits, such as smoking, drinking, or overeating, and he or she continued the habits in spite of the ultimate ramifications? The person would rather die than quit the habits.

We are willing to ruin our lives and the lives of those around us by allowing the ego to control our actions. We are willing to sacrifice our potential for success at work. We are willing to wreck our long-term relationships. When the ego is in complete control, everything worthwhile in our lives is ultimately doomed!

How about family relationships that deteriorated over the years and were never mended? People sometimes go to their deathbeds with grudges, unable to forgive or forget. I have had family members alienate themselves, and we all lost out.

I never met my grandfather on my mom's side, and both grandparents on my dad's side were total strangers to me even though they all lived in close proximity. What an incredible shame! I grew up without ever having these grandparents in my life. They died without forgiving or letting go of whatever drove them away from us. "Whatever it was" ended up being more important than our relationships. Situations like these come down to egos being unable to resolve conflicts.

We still haven't developed a proven way to overcome our egos! We have little to no professional help in this area. It's a real travesty.

I believe that our poor success rates in helping people change destructive behaviors come from the fact that we haven't addressed the role of the ego and its emotions as the major cause of their problems. It's the cause of most troubles in the world! No one is doing anything about it. It's insane!

Addictions of any type can become part of our ego's identity. We can't envision ourselves not doing something because it becomes so ingrained in our behaviors. We identify with the addiction as part of ourselves. Giving something up or changing means giving up part of ourselves. We have emotional attachments with whatever the ego holds onto, even if it is something that might kill us eventually.

Emotional attachments are formed in the lower old mammalian brain where our emotions are held. Once entrenched, holding on to the attachment is part of the ego's need for survival. There are actual neurological connections in the brain for them. Once those pathways are set, so are we!

The thought of losing the ego's attachment becomes fearful. Fear thoughts are centered in the reptilian brain and produce all the brain chemicals that lead to flight-or-fight responses. It's the same thing we talked about in earlier lessons.

The main thing to learn here is that this is why it is so hard to change some of the things we do. If there is an emotional attachment and identification with it, then it becomes a fear response when the possibility of change occurs. Fear stops us dead in our tracks.

Intellectual knowledge without emotional attachment is easily assimilated and readily discarded when new information is presented. It is the emotional ego attachments that have such a hold on us that we can't easily discard habits, routines, and addictions.

We have gone over how the ego is based upon fear. Losing our emotional attachments is scary. What possibly can overcome fear? Let's uncover the greatest of all life lessons.

The Greatest of All Dualities

What I am about to say is so profound, yet so cliché, that I hope my words can come close to conveying what I am attempting to share. It is the answer to many of life's difficult problems that are a result of the ego's fears.

It is responsible for most of the true, meaningful changes that have transformed our lives. Unfortunately, the word I have to use is one of the most overused and abused words in our vocabulary. Its meaning is vastly different from person to person and is misused in so many ways. We hear it almost every day in some way or another; we are probably immune to its importance and its ability to heal and overcome fear.

Some people are incapable of experiencing this miracle because their egos are so powerful that they will not allow it to enter into their lives. When getting what the ego wants is more important than anything else, there is nothing else. Case closed! There are no possibilities.

Without this opposite duality of the ego, relationships are condemned to failure. Without it, marriages fail, parenting is a disaster, business results are less than desired, friendships don't last, and there is no inner peace. In spite of all these negative results, the ego remains in charge of most people in this world who are consumed by getting what they want or getting their way.

So what is the answer to this mystery? I'm sure you have figured this one out. It is, of course, love.

The love-fear duality is at the apex of human nature. Love is the polar opposite of fear. Ego is based upon fear. Real love only lives in the higher self. We have yet to fully understand the significance of this in our lives. Everything we do falls into one of these dualities. Let's first look at love in a slightly different manner in order to begin to understand how it works.

Quite simply, love is letting go of the ego's needs in order to give of our selves to another without any strings attached. Love is present when we can place another's needs above our own. True loves asks for nothing in return. At least, that is my interpretation of it. It is the higher self in action. Volumes of books have been written on love. Songs, poetry, and movies romanticize love—sometimes in unrealistic ways. Love is not just a feeling that overwhelms us.

Falling in love can be one of the greatest of all our experiences, but the kind of love I'm talking about isn't something that happens to us. As we all know, falling in love can be temporary until the ego regains control. At the same time, love isn't something you can just intellectually understand because the feeling component has to be present for love to occur.

Love is a miracle that can occur in our lives. It can create true, long-lasting, meaningful change for us. It only happens when the ego's desires are dropped. That is when love and its miracles take over. Love is not fully present unless there is a giving event and a letting go of the ego's fears. This is where love heals and rewires our lower brains.

Most of us have experienced it in our lives in one way or another. The birth of a child is a profound miracle that can change everything for the people experiencing it.

The symbolic nature of a man and a woman (opposites) joining together with the resulting birth of a child (a miracle) is the best example of how love can recreate and change our lives. No one can explain the depth of love a parent has for a baby until they experience it for themselves.

A marriage of opposites where both partners place the relationship above the ego's needs is another vehicle for the miracle of love that can alter the self. Marriage is one of our greatest classrooms for learning about love.

A death of a loved one is a time when we can place others above our ego's concerns and learn about what love really is. Death changes our perceptions of the world by allowing us the opportunity to lose a part of our lives. We are attached to people we love and cherish. It's only natural and good. They become part of our self-identification. When we lose a loved one, we can't help but lose a part of ourselves.

This may allow us to view life differently. When we can see life differently, we have a chance to expand our awareness. We might finally appreciate and cherish the people around us more. We might be given a chance to trust the process. How big a lesson of love is this?

Losing a parent, spouse, child, relative, or close friend is one of the most traumatic experiences we can go through. After we have sufficiently grieved, we can reflect. Sometimes we learn and grow from the experience. Sometimes we have no choice but to grow.

I have found that life's natural processes of birth, marriage, and death are all here for us to access the higher self through the vehicle of love. Unfortunately, if the ego is too powerful, we lose the ability to experience them in a way that allows love to enter our lives.

I'd Rather Fight Than Switch.

There are many other processes in life that we are thrown into where we can learn and grow. Unfortunately, we don't usually see them as anything other than inconvenient problems that we would rather not deal with. We usually don't have time for nonsense like that. We would rather concentrate on getting the things our egos want out of life.

Instead of learning and growing, we remain stubborn and steadfast in our old ways. Instead of choosing the higher self as the way out of our predicaments, we stand our ground and fight over who is right and who is wrong.

Our egos cannot stand being wrong. They won't tolerate being wrong. Being wrong knocks us off our thrones. How can we be the center of our universe and be wrong? We can't.

Besides, it's so pleasurable and self-validating to be right and to prove others wrong. Now that's good, clean fun. Spouses do it. Parents do it. Bosses do it. Most authoritative figures do it. All of us are guilty of doing it. Why do we enjoy making ourselves right and making others wrong? It makes us feel superior and keeps us firmly ensconced as the reigning supreme rulers of the universe—or at least we know we should be—and everyone else is wrong if they can't see it that way.

Muhammad Ali summed up how most of us really feel about this subject. He said, "I don't always know what I'm talking about, but I know I'm right."

See how our egos work? I know this all too well because that's how my ego works. My ego is just as messed up as everyone else's. I have made all the ego mistakes that are possible in some fashion or another.

But if your ego is at the helm with everything running smoothly and you are winning the games you are playing, then there is a great chance that some of this book might not have the information you are interested in, especially the final lessons. Why change if you are on top of the world?

Everyone is at a different place in life, and some of us are not open to learning new information. Hopefully you have seen the value in what has been presented and will use it to your benefit—and the benefit of those around you. But if you are not ready, all is not lost with this information. Awareness is the first step in learning new information, and now that you have some awareness, it can't be taken away from you. Who knows? Down the road, you might need to use what you have been reading here.

New information and experiences are constantly changing our brain's neural connections. Your brain may have already been altered by the information that has been presented. There has been so much to digest here though; it might be a bit overwhelming.

This Crazy Thing Called Life

This book was written to help people understand and embrace human nature. Now that you have this information, you are one of the privileged few who have solid information about this very obscure, mysterious subject. You have a number of tools to help you get through this crazy thing called life. That's some of the good news.

Life is very mysterious. Life can be a happy, joyous celebration, but it can also become a gut-wrenching, painful torment. The duality of pleasure and pain oscillates in a never-ending cycle that keeps us confused about which parts are real. After learning about duality, you know that both are just as real as the other and dependent upon each other. We need both to be able to experience them fully. Most people would be just fine without the pain, but in keeping with the lessons of duality, you wouldn't be able to really appreciate the pleasure without having pain to contrast it with.

Our world is a masterpiece of creation. Its beauty transcends our abilities to appreciate it, and it's full of aspects that mystify and horrify us. We experience emotions ranging from elation to complacency when the good times are rolling, and when tragedy strikes, we question how a good and compassionate creator could inflict so much pain and suffering upon us.

We have little control over the cycles that shape our lives. At best, we can understand that when the cycle is on the positive side for us, we should know that it won't last forever. When the cycle is negative, we know that good times are right around the corner.

Nothing lasts, and it is unwise to believe that it will. We can create a lot of unnecessary suffering with unrealistic expectations. Expectations are usually symptomatic of being driven by the ego.

We create a lot of unnecessary suffering in our lives in a number of ways, mostly as a result of the adulation of our egos and allowing ourselves to be controlled by its never-ending, self-serving, wanton nature. Life is hard enough sometimes to needlessly make it harder than it is. How we choose to live our lives is up to us. We can choose the path the ego takes us or the path of the higher self.

Philosophers throughout history have pondered human nature and tried to understand this elusive subject. A common thread of thought has been that humankind is ultimately self-serving, down to each individual's wants and needs. I totally agree with this premise. But when one finally realizes that it is not in one's best interest to be self-serving to the ego's wants and needs, it is in their best interests and self-serving to choose the higher self's way of being. By not being self-serving, one chooses a path that ultimately gives us everything we were wanting. This is paradox at its finest!

We all want to be happy, and we make decisions that we believe will take us in that direction. Unfortunately, this thinking process hasn't confirmed that the ways of the ego will not bring long-term happiness. The ego's desire for "getting" is paradoxically the wrong choice if you want to be happy.

Happiness is said to be a choice. I would agree, but a lot has to be present for that choice to be made. I think a lot of internal processing has to go on before someone can choose it. But when one chooses to stop being driven by the ego, the true joy of life can begin. It's up to us to choose the road we want to travel in life. We have been given this gift. We make the choice. That's the best news of all!

How important is relinquishing the ego and accepting the ways of the higher self? The person we have learned so much from, Albert Einstein, thought about it for a while. He said, "We shall require a substantially new way of thinking if humankind is to survive and move toward higher levels."

Wow! That makes it a little more serious and necessary, if you believe him. I do.

For Review

- You are now in possession of proven, scientific, factual information that makes up the T-Code. From this information, you know for certain that each of us is born with a basic temperament that shapes how we think, view the world, and react to others. It basically determines who we are.
- You know for certain that we cannot help being who we are as far as temperament is concerned. Others can't help being who they are any more than we can. In that sense, we are all placed on this earth with different purposes.
- You know for certain that each of us has a valuable place in this world and that we complement each other in an almost magical way, especially those who are opposite from you.
- You know for certain that although your basic temperament will not change, you can acquire some of the skills of other temperaments and overcome some of the weaknesses and limitations of your temperament.
- You know that everyone's temperament is determined by values that are opposite and competing in nature. You know that this creates a world of conflict where your ego-driven perceptions clash with those who don't see it the same way.
- You know that this conflict will never go away, and it is here for a very good reason. It truly is the pathway to choosing higher levels of being.
- You know that the only way out of this senseless conflict is to relinquish the total control of our egos and allow our higher selves to be an active part of our being.

- You know that this is extremely difficult to do because it is totally backward to how we have been living. The ego has survival instincts that are as powerful as any of our emotions.
- You know the fundamentals about our brains and how they function. Research shows us how physical brain functions directly correspond to our temperaments.
- You know that if we don't access the higher self, then the lower, more primitive brains will continue to rule. We are then under the control of impulses that have been created along with our animallike instincts. Our egos are under the influence of these instincts without any choice about its preferences.

Each of these tenets by themselves is capable of changing one's perspective of life. If you can truly grasp one or all of them emotionally and intellectually, you will never be able to see life in the same manner as you used to.

Where do we go now?

The first thing many of us might do with this information is pass it along to people who could really benefit from it. You can give a copy of this book to your spouse, relative, friend, employer, employee, or anybody who constitutes a problem for you from time to time. It might help. But in the end, you have no control over that other person, do you? How hard is it for you to change anything about yourself? It's really hard. And we expect others to do what we can't do ourselves?

I think that it's fair to say that one won't change until the pain of changing is less than the pain of staying where you're at. Until you are really sick and tired of being sick and tired. If life has gotten you down, maybe that's a good thing. Maybe it's an opportunity to make a positive change. Problems create the environment for us to change.

We are sometimes tempted to want to change others—sometimes for very good reasons—but people have to go through their own special experiences in order to grow. It's all out of our control. Sometimes we just have to trust the process.

We can alter the process with our awareness in life-changing ways. When we accept people for whom they are—without judgment or condemnation—this gesture can actually act as a catalyst that wires their brains to be able to accept others (maybe even us) who may believe differently than they do.

Think of the ramifications if people started accepting the differences of others. How would you feel if others accepted you for who you are? Acceptance can only occur if we can give up control and judgment of others. A huge byproduct of acceptance is that we will not enter into conflict with others. Acceptance is a part of love that can make miracles occur. Good things can happen when we aren't creating negative reactions in others. We can affect life in so many different ways.

A Grand Conclusion

With all this information, we still need to have a conclusion that will bring our earthly experience into a simple, clear, concise summation. After years of consideration, I finally came up with these thoughts. In my humble opinion, I feel like the mystery of life and human nature can be wrapped up in just a few sentences:

- This world is a stage of endless conflicts of duality. These conflicts are the source of all of our drama, trauma, suffering, and confusion.
- The reason for our conflict is our egos. Our egos have opposing and competing values in their natures. There is no solution to problems created by our egos when we use our egos to solve them. There is no use trying to repeat the same tactics. It's insanity!
- The solutions to our conflicts are paradoxically opposite to our normal ways of thinking, which are set by our egos. We have to act in a way that is uncomfortable and foreign to our egos. Real solutions are only found at a higher level of self.
- Our problems are pathways to the higher self. What gives us so much pain will ultimately help us grow. What we try to avoid at all costs holds the answers to the most important questions in our lives.

After I wrote these four sentences about the mystery of life, I remembered something about a saying from Buddhism: "Life is suffering." It seemed similar to my first summary sentence. I felt compelled to look it up. When I found the source of the saying, I literally got goose bumps. This saying was the first of four truths that are central to Buddhism. The four sentences I wrote that described the mystery of life are almost identical to the Four Noble Truths of Buddha, which were formulated more than 2,500 years ago in northeastern India.

It was extremely validating to arrive at the same conclusions about life as Buddha. This gives a bit of credibility to the thought process I used to write this book. I think that it adds a nice finishing touch to this journey through the mysteries of human nature.

Thank you for reading this book

So there you have it. The mysteries of human nature have been revealed and dissected like never before. The possibilities of understanding yourself, others, and our interactions are all here for you—if you are interested. I hope that you are.

I want to thank you for spending your valuable time and energy reading this book. Writing a book on this subject was a daunting project. Honestly, I didn't know if I could pull it off. But I plowed through, supported by the fact that it really needed to be written by someone. My motivation was to help others recognize this amazing information that I was fortunate to have stumbled across. It was important enough to me to put it down on paper. I believe this information has been unknown by most people for long enough.

My sincere wish is for this book to have been of benefit to you in uncovering and clarifying some of the mysteries of human nature. Awareness is always the first step for learning new information. If you can understand the concepts, expect good things to happen. Once you create an intention to start using this material, you are on your way. If you can master even a portion, it will open a whole new world of possibilities. Your life will never be the same. I promise!

That is my intention for you.

May your journey from here lead you to pursue the mastery of this mystery called life. Good luck and Godspeed!

The lessons we're learning,

As these pages keep turning.

This trial and tribulation,

Will give way to elation.

The pain we relive,

We'll forget and forgive.

We gaze at the heavens,

As our earthly bread leavens.

There is hope for salvation,

Our soul's liberation.

The higher self will birth it.

In the end, it's all worth it.

Postscript

Whoever was responsible for the idea of dividing self into lower and higher parts committed a crime against humanity. This division has given rise to the notion that the lower (ego and immature) self must be overcome while the higher (unitive and whole) self must be sought as the goal of human realization. Out of ignorance, I too clung to this notion because I believed it was this higher self that would be united with God for all eternity. It took a long time before my experiences led me to doubt this conviction and, at the same time, let in the possibility that this was not the whole truth and there was still further to go.
—Bernadette Roberts, *The Experience of No-Self*

Bernadette Roberts was a nun for the Carmelite order for ten years. She sees the higher self as just a first milestone in our journeys. The next milestone she refers to is the "no-self" event, the ending of all "self-consciousness," and the revelation of what remains beyond self.

I don't doubt her a bit, but it is too far ahead of where I am to deal with this possibility. I believe that she is saying there is something after duality—that duality exists in this physical world but not in the spiritual world.

After the earthly experience, after our bodies have been used and discarded, the duality thing may no longer be necessary. She does validate the fact that while we are here on earth we have the higher and lower self to contend with, but after all this, there is much more. The journey continues.

Random Quotes On Human Nature

It's a wonder that I haven't dropped all my ideals, because they seem so absurd and impossible to carry out. Yet I keep them, because in spite of everything, I still believe that people are really good at heart.

—Anne Frank, *The Diary of a Young Girl*

I have no faith in human perfectability. I think that human exertion will have no appreciable effect upon humanity. Man is now only more active—not more happy—nor more wise, than he was 6,000 years ago.

—Edgar Allan Poe, *Letter to J. R. Lowell*

What small potatoes we all are, compared with what we might be!

—Charles Dudley Warner, *My Summer in a Garden*

If we could read the secret history of our enemies, we should find in each man's life sorrow and suffering enough to disarm all hostilities.

—Henry Wadsworth Longfellow, *Driftwood*

There's only one corner of the universe you can be certain of improving, and that's your own self.

—Aldous Huxley, *Time Must Have a Stop*

Most people don't believe something can happen until it already has. That's not stupidity or weakness, that's just human nature.

—Max Brooks, *World War Z: An Oral History of the Zombie War*

Nature never appeals to intelligence until habit and instinct are useless. There is no intelligence where there is no need to change.

—H. G. Wells, *The Time Machine*

Change is one of the scariest things in the world and yet it is also one of those variables of human existence that no one can avoid.

—Aberjhani, *Journey through the Power of the Rainbow: Quotations from a Life Made out of Poetry*

No passion is stronger in the breast of a man than the desire to make others believe as he believes. Nothing so cuts at the root of his happiness and fills him with rage as the sense that another rates low what he prizes highly.

—Virginia Woolf, *Orlando*

Avoidable human misery is more often caused not so much by stupidity as by ignorance, particularly our ignorance about ourselves.

—Carl Sagan, *The Demon-Haunted World: Science as a Candle in the Dark*

One is fruitful, only at the cost of being rich in contradictions.

—Friedrich Nietzsche, *Twilight of the Idols*

Forget dice rolling or boxes of chocolates as metaphors for life. Think of yourself as a dreaming robot on autopilot, and you will be much closer to the truth.

—Albert-László Barabasi, *Bursts: The Hidden Pattern behind Everything We Do*

One man's gospel truth is another man's blasphemous lie. The dangerous thing about people is the way we'll try to kill anyone whose truth doesn't agree with ours.

—Mira Grant, *Blackout*

No one has yet determined the power of the human species ... what it may perform by instinct, and what it may accomplish with rational determination.

—Brian Herbert, *House Harkonnen*

I have an unshakable belief that mankind's higher nature is on the whole still dormant. The greatest souls reveal excellencies of mind and heart which their lesser fellows possess—hidden, it is true, but there all the time.

—Helen Keller, *Let Us Have Faith*

The science of Human Nature has never been attempted as the science of Nature has. The dry light has never shone on it. Neither physics nor metaphysics have touched it.

—Henry David Thoreau, *Journal, 15 June 1840*

We are single cells in a body of four billion cells. The body is humankind. I glory in the miracle of self, but my individuality does not separate me from the oneness of humanity.

—Norman Cousins, *Human Options: An Autobiographical Notebook*

We are all Christ; we're all Hitler.

—John Lennon, *Bed-In for Peace* interview

There is a design for all humanity, which will be manifested only as humanity becomes a whole, a design which will make clear all that has gone before.

—N. Sri Ram, *Thoughts for Aspirants*

He who has so little knowledge of human nature as to seek happiness by changing anything but his own disposition will waste his life in fruitless efforts and multiply the grief he proposes to remove.

—Samuel Johnson, *The Rambler*

He who knows no hardships will know no hardihood. He who faces no calamity will need no courage. Mysterious though it is, the characteristics in human nature which we love best grow in a soil with a strong mixture of troubles.

—Henry Emerson Fosdick, *The Christian Herald* (1969), Volume 92, page 72

True happiness for human beings is possible only to those who develop their godlike potentialities to the utmost.

—Bertrand Russell, *The Conquest of Happiness*

To feel much for others and little for ourselves: to restrain our selfishness and exercise our benevolent affections, constitute the perfection of human nature.

—Adam Smith, *The Theory of Moral Sentiments*

Human Nature is the only science of man: and yet has been hitherto the most neglected.

—David Hume, *A Treatise of Human Nature*

No tendency is quite so strong in human nature as the desire to lay down rules of conduct for other people.

—William Howard Taft, Quoted in Robert J Schoenberg (1992), *Mr. Capone*

Man has demonstrated that he is master of everything—except his own nature.

—Henry Miller, *The Air-Conditioned Nightmare*

Men go to far greater lengths to avoid what they fear than to obtain what they desire.

—Dan Brown, *The Da Vinci Code*

Why do you have to be the same as the others? …Most of them are stupid.

—Ken Follett, *Winter of the World*

Of all the forces in the universe, the hardest to overcome is the force of habit.

—Terry Pratchett, *Johnny and the Dead*

We must take human nature as we find it, perfection falls not to the share of mortals.

—George Washington, Letter to John Jay

We compound our suffering by victimizing each other.

—Athol Fugard, *The Observer*

The ultimate measure of a man is not where he stands in moments of comfort, but where he stands at times of challenge and controversy.

—Martin Luther King, *Strength to Love*

We do not escape our boundaries or our innermost being. We do not change. It is true we may be transformed, but we will always walk within our boundaries, within the marked-off circle.

—Ernest Junger, *The Glass Bees*

Our mind is capable of passing beyond the dividing line we have drawn for it. Beyond the pairs of opposites of which the world consists, other, new insights begin.

—Hermann Hesse, *Stories of Five Decades*

Hate the sin and not the sinner is a precept which, though easy enough to understand, is rarely practiced, and that is why the poison of hatred spreads in the world.

—Mahatma Gandhi, *An Autobiography: The Story of My Experiments with the Truth*

Holding anger is a poison. It eats you from the inside. We think that hating is a weapon that attacks the person that harmed us. But hatred is a curved blade. And the harm we do, we do to ourselves.

—Mitch Albom, *The Five People You Meet in Heaven*

We cannot live only for ourselves. A thousand fibers connect us with our fellow men; and among those fibers, as sympathetic threads, our actions run as causes, and they come back to us as effects.

—Rev. Henry Melville, *Golden Lectures*

Appendix

More about You, Us, and Them

Knowing yourself is the beginning of all wisdom.
—Aristotle

Here in a short, easy-to-identify format are descriptions of the sixteen temperament types. Of course, many books have been written about these types, and I encourage you to read them for more details. It is my aim to summarize and simplify this information in a way this powerful and compelling information deserves. In short, I want to spread the word to the world.

Please be advised that I have borrowed liberally from the wonderful work that has been done and express my profound admiration and appreciation for those who did it. All I have done in this appendix is to group the types differently than previous authors. I believe it brings balance and symmetry so that it may be understood more readily.

As you have seen in earlier lessons, use of the first two dualities (feelers versus thinkers and inners versus outers) produced our four basic groups:

- amiables
- expressives
- analyticals
- drivers

Then, I added two more dualities (nowers versus planners and flexers versus controllers)—the great subdivide—to further define each of these basic groups into four subgroups and reveal the sixteen temperament types that define us all. These sixteen types have been described and labeled as most recognized by the Myers-Briggs classification of temperament types.

The point of going over each of the types is so that each of you reading this lesson might have the opportunity to better find yourself within this framework. I feel it is so important that I will continue to say it is the beginning of mastering human nature.

The Amiables

As we have mentioned before, people are the most important aspect of life to an amiable. They're born to help others, are friendly and easy to be with, and they are very good at building relationships. The four types of amiables are discussed here. The Myers-Briggs labels are included underneath my descriptions if you want to look them up for further reference.

Adaptive Amiables
(Myers-Briggs INFP)

They put a high priority on restoring unity, integrity, and oneness. With a deep sense of idealism and a firm belief in conciliation, caring, and selflessness, they are deeply committed to the common good. Often called *healers*, they are dedicated to mending divisions in their personal and private lives. Comprising less than 3 percent of the population, their idealism often leaves them feeling isolated from the rest of humanity. They are attracted to careers that allow them to be moral and altruistic, such as the ministry, missionary work, and social work. They are comfortable working alone and are not suited for careers in business.

Impulsive Amiables
Myers-Briggs ISFP

With an extraordinary ability to work with the slightest nuances of color, tone, texture, aroma, and flavor, people of this temperament bring synthesis to any aspect in the world of senses. They have a special talent for tactical artistry. Both friendly and unconditionally kind people, they highly value freedom and conversely dislike routine. Called *composers,* these creative and sensual types love to create beauty and pleasure for the enjoyment of others. At 10 percent of the population, they are drawn to a variety of careers, such as decorative design, fashion designers, film directors, and food preparation.

Strategic Amiables
Myers-Briggs INFJ

Here are individuals with a strong desire to contribute to others by helping them realize their full potential. Private and sensitive, they are excellent listeners. Although reserved, they are empathetic with extraordinary imaginations, personal warmth, insight, and devotion. They have unusually vivid inner lives and quietly exert their influence behind the scenes with family, friends, and others. Called *counselors,* they enjoy guiding their companions toward greater personal fulfillment. As 2–3 percent of the population, they choose to become therapists, psychologists, psychiatrists, and physicians. They also teach or write in those fields.

Authoritative Amiables
Myers-Briggs ISFJ

While the primary goal of these people is to be of service to others, it is directed toward guarding others against life's pitfalls and perils. They are warmhearted and sympathetic—with an extraordinary sense of safety, security, and responsibility. They give happily of themselves to those in need, although their interest may wane when their recipient is no longer in trouble. Loyal and devoted to their superiors, they are impressed with social order. They believe in the safety of traditional social hierarchy and strive to uphold custom and tradition. As *protectors,* they constitute about 10 percent of the population. They do well as curators, librarians, private secretaries, middle managers, and nurses.

The Expressives

Confident and hedonistic, these individuals are spontaneous, highly verbal, and not at all troubled by the fact that they are somewhat disorganized and easily sidetracked. But through it all, they're fun to be around.

Adaptive Expressives
Myers-Briggs ENFP

Tireless and enthusiastic conversationalists, these people have an irrepressible expressive nature. They have a strong drive to speak out on social issues and events, inspiring others to join their causes. Fiercely independent, they repudiate any kind of subordination. They're keen observers of others, hypersensitive, hyper-alert, and always ready for emergencies. With outstanding intuitive powers, they are able to interpret hidden motives in the words and actions of others. Called *champions,* they constitute only 2–3 percent of the population. In the workforce, they are warmly enthusiastic, imaginative, and highly spirited. They make excellent teachers and ministers and have a natural interest in journalism and public speaking.

Impulsive Expressives
Myers-Briggs ESFP

As natural entertainers and performers, these individuals are fun, loving, and playful. They radiate warmth and festivity. Not surprising, they're lively, witty, and enjoy entertaining while hating anxiety and anything to do with the gloomy and the serious. They seek stimulation and sensation. For them, life is a party. The way they see it, if it's not fun and exciting, it's not worth doing. Appropriately called *performers,* they love to get others together to lighten up and cast off their worries and cares. As 10 percent of the population, they are drawn to careers in sales, real estate, and public relations.

Strategic Expressives
Myers-Briggs ESFJ

Natural-born teachers, they make people their highest priority. They seem to have an uncanny ability to influence others and inspire them with their enthusiasm. Very caring and concerned, they are primarily interested in the growth and development of others. These outgoing types exhibit a willingness to become involved with others on a regular basis. Called *teachers,* they have a highly developed talent to empathize with people. As 2–3 percent of the population, they make wonderful educators, primary care physicians, ministers, sales executives, and media professionals.

Authoritative Expressives
Myers-Briggs ESFJ

These types are concerned with providing others with the material necessities of life. As such, they are eager to serve others in many ways. Very social, they value cooperation, and social facilitation is imperative to them. They are the masters of ceremony and are great with details involved in arranging goods and services. To make sure the needs of others are met, that traditions are followed, and social functions are a success, they give happily of their time and energy. Called *providers,* they make up about 10 percent of the population. They lean toward service organizations, sales, teaching, coaching, personal secretaries, and receptionists.

The Analyticals

Here is the factual, logical, and stoic branch of the human family. These individuals are less concerned with people and more connected with the physical world and the technical. As such, they're good listeners and handle complexity well. As a *strategic analytical,* I can obviously relate to this group the most.

Adaptive Analyticals
Myers-Briggs INTP

Designers of systemic structures and engineering structural designs, these masters of organization prize intelligence. They have the greatest precision in thought and language of all types. Actually, they look upon the world as little more than raw material to be reshaped to their designs. External reality is unimportant except to be checked out for the usefulness of ideas. Called *architects,* they seem constantly on the lookout for the technological principles and natural laws upon which the world is structured. Only 1–3 percent of the population, they are the architects, mathematicians, logicians, systems analysts, and structural designers.

Impulsive Analyticals
Myers-Briggs ISTP

The outstanding characteristic of members of this temperament type is the masterful operation and handling of tools, equipment, and instrumentation of all kinds. At an early age, they are drawn to tools, and they feel a need to manipulate them. They are spontaneous and enjoy doing their own thing—unrestricted by rules, regulations, or laws. Fearless risk-takers who are drawn to excitement, they can be insubordinate. Called *crafters,* they like pitting themselves or their techniques against chance or the odds. Making up 10 percent of the population, these soft-spoken, hard-bitten, action-oriented people choose a variety of occupations from tradesman, carpenters, mechanics, and plumbers to pilots, surgeons, athletes, musicians, and military members.

Strategic Analyticals
Myers-Briggs INTJ

People of this type choose to study science or technology and work with systems. They excel in contingency planning and developing theoretical models that can be translated into reality. They are the most confident and independent of all with a powerful will to achieve. Called *masterminds,* they love to respond to solving problems that require creative solutions. Comprising less than 3 percent of the population, these reclusive people usually rise to positions of responsibility. They choose scientific fields in which to work where they can build data and human systems, or they can be business executives.

Authoritative Analyticals
Myers-Briggs ISTJ

Earnest and attentive in inspecting products and the accounts of institutions, these types usually work behind the scenes to ensure against irregularities or discrepancies. Normally reporting to higher authorities, they do their work without fanfare. As a result, their dedication can go unnoticed and unappreciated. These hard-nosed, conservative people are interested in details, thoroughness, and accuracy. Called *inspectors,* they are super-dependable in everything they do. As 10 percent of the population, they make excellent bank examiners, auditors, accountants, investment managers, tax attorneys, dentists, optometrists, law researchers, legal secretaries, and teachers.

The Drivers

These practical, pragmatic, and task-oriented people are quick to make decisions. It's their way or the highway. They're highly organized, direct in their dealings, and devoted to the bottom line. Welcome the *drivers*—they get things done in this world.

Adaptive Drivers
Myers-Briggs ENTP

People of this temperament type build prototypes, ingenious gadgets, and other mechanisms to make systems more efficient. They are reluctant to do anything in a particular manner and are preoccupied with science and technology. With an engaging entrepreneurial spirit, they hate conforming to rules and regulations while enjoying total freedom of action. They have an insatiable hunger for knowledge that allows them to work for better ways to do almost anything. They're good at both functional analysis and engineering human relationships. Called *inventors,* they comprise less than 3 percent of the population. They usually work as entrepreneurs or in research, but they can also be outstanding teachers.

Impulsive Drivers
Myers-Briggs ESTP

They are adept at putting forward an enterprise and getting people to go along with what they propose. Their sheer confidence seems to persuade others. Witty, clever, and fun to be with, they have a knack for knowing where the action is. They also seem to have a hearty appetite for the finer things in life. Called *promoters,* they have an unusual ability to win people over, and they are willing to do whatever it takes to achieve their goals. At 10 percent of the population, they are sharp entrepreneurs, bold defense lawyers, industrialists, real estate developers, and high-powered sales executives.

Strategic Drivers
Myers-Briggs ENTJ

These people are the natural-born leaders of the world. Frank and decisive, they are great mobilizers of people and command others with their strength and power. They have a strong natural urge to bring order and efficiency to an organization. Marshaling personnel and material to meet specified goals is their specialty. Called *field marshals,* they make up only 1–3 percent of the population. Their career choices usually include the military, business, education, and government.

Authoritative Drivers
Myers-Briggs ESTJ

Members of this group are eager to enforce the rules and regulations of an organization. They are highly materialistic and follow standard operating procedures as a guide for living. As social and civic-minded individuals, they are usually pillars of the community. Called *supervisors,* they make sure things are done the right way. They expect others to share the same values and have little to no patience or understanding of those who don't. At 10 percent of the population, they are good at scheduling orderly procedures and evaluating others in their performances. For career opportunities, they are interested in commerce, corporate law, politics, business, police work, and military service.

Now You Know

If you're like most people, you probably have one of two reactions to everything covered so far. Either it all makes sense (and you already have a darn good idea what your basic temperament is), or there are so many variables here that you're just not sure what your temperament is.

For some of us, it's not all that easy to figure out who we really are temperament-wise because there are traits in the great subdivide that correspond to the traits of the four basic groups. This can make it confusing, especially if you have opposing and contradicting traits in your type.

Types like the authoritative amiables, the strategic expressives, the adaptive drivers, and the impulsive analyticals all have contradicting and opposing traits embedded in their temperaments that may confuse the discovery process.

Having a hard time figuring it all out? Here is a suggestion that might help. Pick out the best types that seem to describe you. Go on the Internet and search for what you believe to be your Myers-Briggs designation. For example, if you feel like you are an ESFP, just type that into your browser and do a search. Many articles and sites will come up for you to read.

This will produce a wealth of information on that particular temperament type. If reviewing that material indicates that's not the real you, try the next one that might fit you until you discover the one that describes you perfectly.

I included this information because I believe it is critical to know yourself if you are ever going to master this thing called life. Nothing else matters unless you figure out your strengths, your weaknesses, and where you naturally fit into this world. It might be difficult to have a true appreciation of yourself and others without this kind of knowledge. Hopefully this book will help you in your awakening.

I implore you to further your investigation of this vital subject by reading and studying more about it. Socrates agreed when he said, "Know thyself!"

The last summary poem will be dedicated to helping you understand the value of all this:

The beginning will begin
With understanding your being.
Knowing the real you,
Finding what you weren't seeing,

Unleashing your passion.
It was there all along.
You just covered it over,
Not knowing where you belong.

They said get a good job
To pay all your bills
Only concerned with a paycheck
Seeking material thrills.

That's missing the point.
You have a mission on earth.
When you find it, all of life changes.
You will experience a new birth

When you do what was destined
With your gifts from the spirit.
You'll finally see the light
And will start moving near it.

References

Damasio, A. R. *Descartes' Error: Emotion, Reason, and the Human Brain*. New York: Putnam, 1994.

Descartes, R. *Discourse On Method*. New York: Bartleby.com, 1637/2001.

Ekman, P., and R. J. Davidson. *The Nature of Emotion*. New York: Oxford University Press, 1994.

Glasser, W. *Choice Theory*. New York: HarperCollins, 1999.

Jung, C. *Psychological Types*. Princeton, New Jersey: Princeton Press, 1971.

Hill, N. *Law of Success*. Meriden, Connecticut: The Ralston University Press, 1928.

Hobbes, T. *Leviathan*. New York: Oxford University Press, 1651/1957

Keirsey, D., and M. Bates. *Please Understand Me*. Del Mar, California: Prometheus Books, 1978.

LaDoux, J. *The Emotional Brain*. New York: Simon and Schuster, 1998.

Locke, J. *An Essay Concerning Human Understanding*. New York: Dutton, 1690/1947.

MacLean, P. *The Triune Brain in Evolution*. New York: Springer, 1990.

McDonald, J. H. *Tao Te Ching* (translation for public domain). www.wright-house.com.

Merrill, D. W., and R. Reid. *Personal Styles and Effective Performance*. Boca Raton, Florida: CRC Press, 1981.

Pinker, S. *The Blank Slate*. New York: Viking Penguin, 2002.

Pirsig, R. *Zen And The Art Of Motorcycle Maintenance*. New York: HarperCollins, 1974.

Quinn, R., and K. Cameron. *Diagnosing and Changing Organizational Culture*. Reading: Addison-Wesley, 1999.

Rouseau, J. *Discourse upon the Original Foundation of Inequality*. New York: Oxford University Press, 1755/1994.

Schucman, H. *A Course in Miracles*. New York: Viking, The Foundation for Inner Peace, 1976.

Zeithaml, V. A. *Delivering Quality Service*. New York: The Free Press, 1990.

TRUE DIRECTIONS
An affiliate of Tarcher Books

OUR MISSION

Tarcher's mission has always been to publish books that contain great ideas. Why? Because:

GREAT LIVES BEGIN WITH GREAT IDEAS

At Tarcher, we recognize that many talented authors, speakers, educators, and thought-leaders share this mission and deserve to be published – many more than Tarcher can reasonably publish ourselves. True Directions is ideal for authors and books that increase awareness, raise consciousness, and inspire others to live their ideals and passions.

Like Tarcher, True Directions books are designed to do three things:
inspire, inform, and motivate.

Thus, True Directions is an ideal way for these important voices to bring
their messages of hope, healing, and help to the world.

Every book published by True Directions– whether it is non-fiction, memoir, novel,
poetry or children's book – continues Tarcher's mission to publish works that
bring positive change in the world. We invite you to join our mission.

For more information, see the True Directions website:
www.iUniverse.com/TrueDirections/SignUp

Be a part of Tarcher's community to bring positive change in this world! See exclusive author videos, discover new and exciting books, learn about upcoming events, connect with author blogs and websites, and more!
www.tarcherbooks.com

TRUE DIRECTIONS
AN AFFILIATE OF TARCHER BOOKS

Printed in the United States
By Bookmasters